P9-CBC-562

Extraordinary Play with Ordinary Things

Extraordinary Play with Ordinary Things

Barbara Sher, M.A., O.T.R.

Illustrations: Janet Young

BOB ADAMS, INC.
Holbrook, Massachusetts

Copyright ©1994, Barbara Sher. All rights reserved. This book, or parts thereof, may not be reproduced in any form without permission from the publisher; exceptions are made for brief excerpts used in published reviews.

Published by Bob Adams, Inc.
260 Center Street, Holbrook, MA 02343

ISBN: 1-55850-406-0

Printed in the United States of America.

J I H G F E D C B A

Library of Congress Cataloging-in-Publication Data

Sher, Barbara
        Extraordinary play with ordinary things : make-it-yourself, do-it-yourself
activities that encourage your child's development / Barbara Sher.
                p.   cm.
        Originally published: Tucson : Therapy Skill Builders, c 1992.
        Includes bibliographical references and index.
        ISBN 1-55850-406-0
        1. Movement education. 2. Games. 3. Games—Equipment and supplies. 4.
Motor learning. I. Title.
[GV452.S56 1994]
372.86ROCESS—dc20

This publication is designed to provide accurate and authoritative information with regard to the subject matter covered. It is sold with the understanding that the publisher is not engaged in rendering legal, accounting, or other professional advice. If legal advice or other expert assistance is required, the services of a competent professional person should be sought.
— From a *Declaration of Principles* jointly adopted by a Committee of the American Bar Association and a Committee of Publishers and Associations

COVER DESIGN: Barry Littmann

In 1992, Therapy Skills Builders, 3830 East Bellevue, Tucson, Arizona, originally published a version of this book that emphasized the therapeutic aspects of the games. This publication was a resource book for therapists, teachers, and other professionals.

This book is available at quantity discounts for bulk purchases.
For information, call 1-800-872-5627.

Persons using this book and engaging in the activities therein accept the responsiblity to closely monitor all activities involving children. The publisher assumes no liability for any accident, injury, or mishap that may arise from the activities described in this book.

This book is dedicated to the extraordinary people in my very own family, Richard, Roxanne and Marissa.

Table of Contents

Acknowledgments

To acknowledge the people who helped me with this book is to acknowledge the people who are in my life, beginning with my family. Thanks to Richard, my partner for twenty-four years, who says the secret to a long-lasting relationship is a patient man—and who proves it with his calm nature. Our daughters Roxanne and Marissa have been more than an inspiration to me; they helped create this book with their endless supply of ideas for games and activities. My thanks likewise go out to the children who played with me at Whitethorn, Redway, Skyfish, and Whale Gulch elementary schools and at Children House preschool in northern California, as well as the preschool children at the Peer Program in Saipan, Northern Mariana Islands, and the Head Start Program in Palau, another Micronesian island. Thanks, too, to the therapists, teachers, and parents who played games with me at my workshops in the States, Hong Kong, Saipan, New Zealand, Fiji, and Rarotonga.

Thanks also go to my good friend Joan Becker, who came up with the name for this book and who, along with dear friends Lorraine Carolan and Cindy Taylor, is a loving source of support for my dreams.

I am grateful, finally, to my late father, my mom, and my brother and sisters, who encouraged my writing by pretending to get excited about the homemade birthday cards I always made them.

About this book

I WROTE THIS BOOK because I could never find a ball when I needed one. Not that one wasn't around. A ball would invariably appear under the bed or on the bottom shelf or behind the door whenever we weren't looking for one. It was only when the inspiration to play ball would come that the ball would seem to go.

I wrote this book as a response to those days, living with small children, when I became acutely aware that their bodies were vibrating at a greater number of revolutions per second than mine. Sometimes the difference between our energy levels was enough to make me want to run out of the house. Instead, I'd take some long deep breaths and remind myself that I really did love being a mother and in ten years, this moment will be funny. This worked for me.

I wrote this book because, like you, I am nuts about my kids and I want to do what's best for them. Because for the last twenty-five years I've been an occupational therapist working with children who are delayed in their development, I've acquired a sense of what activities best benefit a child's development. You'll find that the games and activities in this book benefit children as well as delighting them.

Finally, I wrote this book because it's so satisfying in today's world to find a good use for things that usually get added to the rubbish pile. So here are over seven hundred games, well tested by children and often made up by children, that are good for children and fun to do with children and that, if a ball is needed, require nothing more than a few sheets of newspaper!

Here is an example of one game.

Picture this scene: It's raining. The morning went fairly smoothly, but you are starting to hear an edge in the children's voices. Words like "Did not" and "Did too" are starting to rise in volume, shrilling in your ears. Do

you yell and add your decibels, or do you try and find another way?

Another way: Start taping newspaper sections down on the floor. Make sure they see you, but don't tell them why; just say it's a secret or a surprise. When you've taped four or five or them, challenge them to a game.

"Can you jump from one section to another? Wonderful! Can you jump sideways? Fantastic! How about backward? Whoa! That's tricky, isn't it? How about jumping over two of them? Great try! Can you hop on each one? Wow, I am impressed! Can you hop sideways? Terrific! How else can you jump or hop on them? Clever.

"Now I am going to mark the first one with the number "1" and the second one with a number "2," and here is "3," "4," and "5." I want you to jump from "1" to "3," backwards to "2," and then all the way to "5"!"

Obviously you will have to make up the challenge to fit your child's abilities, but that is the beauty of a game like this. Children of various skill levels and ages can all play together. I've played these games in main-streamed classrooms in such a way that the peers of the child I was working with as well as the child himself—the child whose motor skills were less developed than others in his class—could join in the fun together.

"Josh," I might say, if Josh is the kind of born ath-lete who loves physical challenges and will be disruptive to others if he is bored, "you jump to every other one doing a complete twirl in the air before you land."

To Jennifer I might say, knowing she is a little unsure of her body, "I want you to jump from one to the other holding both arms in the air at the same time," making Jennifer feel that her two-part direction is as complicated as Josh's.

Sometimes I have let the children who are standing in line make up directions for each other. This works best if the person right behind the one whose turn it is makes up the direction, ensuring that everyone gets a turn to move and a turn to talk. (You can also slyly set up who is behind whom.)

If you are playing with more than three children —and this is definitely the kind of game that neighbor kids will love—have them stand in a line facing the newspaper sections rather than standing behind each other. Having children stand behind each other is the same as inviting them to wrestle and push. Standing beside each other, facing the action, allows them to be a part of what's happening.

I doubt you need reminding that praise is always wonderful to hear. I have a dance teacher who always finds something positive to say, no matter what we do. I don't even care whether it's true; it just feels good to be cheered on.

And by the way, don't worry if you can't find any tape. If the sections aren't taped down, they'll slip and slide some, but that will just intensify the elements of balance and motor planning in the game. This conveniently leads me to my next subject: what skills are being learned in these games.

The fun games in this book are "good for children" because they develop skills that help children move well and even do better academically. For example, kids who get their "b's" and "d's" confused because they can't remember which side the line goes on may not have developed an internal sense of "sidedness." "Sidedness" is the ability to move each side of the body completely independently from the other. Kicking and hopping games and other one-sided activities, increase this sense. Once a child has a good internal awareness of how her body works, she can apply that knowledge to the external world.

Know that motoric development happens sequentially. Although there are exceptions, it is generally best for children to follow the natural sequences of motor development, doing movements such as crawling before walking, jumping before hopping, and hopping before skipping. Check the list of sequential stages of motor development in the glossary. You may even find a area or two of your own that your children can help you with!

How to Use This Book

This book has over seven hundred ideas for games, so don't make yourself crazy trying to remember them. I suggest browsing through the book at first and jotting down any of the ideas that appeal to you or fit your children's needs. I have tried to put in a wide selection.

We all have different tastes and tempos, and an activity that seems too wild (or too slow) for one person may feel just right for another. Some may feel just right for a slow, lazy day and others better for the high-energy times—or for the days when you want to decrease their high energy somewhat! You might want to divide the list in two. One side could include high energy games like "jumping through hoops" (yes, there really is a game like that in chapter 4), and the other side could have quiet games like "ball flick," where you scrunch up tiny balls of newspaper and see how far you can flick them.

Or you might just want to jot down ideas that go with one kind of material. Say you have a bag of aluminum cans that you are ready to take to the recycling center. Let the kids have an afternoon of can games, from bowling them down to stacking, kicking, and squashing them, and *really* get some use out of them!

Do plan to introduce a few games in one play period. Some games will "take" and last for a while, and some won't depending upon the mood and energy level of the day.

After you have browsed through the book and jotted down the ideas that appeal to you, stick them on your refrigerator. Then when the moment feels right for playing games, you won't have to be mumbling, "What were those ideas I liked anyway?" To keep things fresh, jot down a few more another day.

At the back of the book I have included a list of motor skills and a list of the ages at which most children

are able to perform key activities. You can use this to give you a sense of how one skill builds on another. If you wish to make some aspects of your child's development stronger, check the glossary for an explanation of the basic skills and then the index for the appropriate games.

And now let the games begin . . .

Games to play with newspapers

NEWSPAPERS ARE IN limitless supply. If you don't want to read one first, go to the nearest post office and you'll find their wastebaskets full of advertising newspapers that are sent free through the mail and thrown away by box holders. You might feel like a bag lady going through the wastebaskets, but it's for a good cause!

One of the nice things about playing with balls made of scrunched-up newspapers is that the "balls" are very light, requiring only a little strength to manipulate. And children will not be afraid to be hit with them.

NEWSPAPER GAMES FOR ONE OR MORE PLAYERS

Square Jumps

Lay a newspaper square down to mark the start. Call this square "home" and explain that each game begins from "home." Lay a second square down in front of "home" and have the player jump over the second square. Then lay a third square in front of the second one and have the player jump over both at once. Continue adding a square one at a time and see how many squares your player can jump over. Remember the number and see whether she can jump further the next time you play.

> *I know newspaper sections are really rectangular in shape, but I am calling them "squares" because squares is easier to say.*

Leap the Squares

This is like Square Jumps, except that the player leaps over the squares. (Jumps land on two feet; leaps land on one.) There are two ways to do the leaping. One is to take a running start and then leap. The other is to leap from a standstill directly in front of the squares. Try both ways.

Square Lines

Lay a number of newspaper sections in a straight line, each square a small distance from the other. Ask your player to stand on "home" and then jump from one square to the next, down to the end of the line. Next have the player jump sideways down the line of squares, then backwards. Have the player hop them, first with his right and then with his left leg. Ask him to jump to every other square or, if appropriate, every third one.

Academic Squares

Number the squares (1, 2, 3 . . .) with a large dark marker. Lay the squares out sequentially or randomly and ask the children to jump from one square to another; for example, from one to three. If the numbers are not placed

sequentially, the jump from one to two might be easy, but the one from two to three a real doozy. Or use the alphabet, asking children to jump from A to B, etc., or to the letters that their name starts with or spells. Call out the sequence to be jumped beforehand, like the word CAT or a nonsense sequence such as DDFA, and see whether they can remember the sequence and do the jumps in order.

I like including academic skills in motor games because children are still learning through their bodies. These kinds of games reinforce their school work in a way that is fun and natural for them. Asking the child's teachers what academic work needs reinforcing earns appreciation from the teacher and continuity for the child. Remembering sequences will help them with math, science, and spelling.

You can also work on prepositions by asking the child to stand **on** his or her square and then to stand **beside** it, stand **over** it (straddle), jump **off** it, go **around** it, and finally go **under** it.

Solitaire

Using a deck of cards and a section of newspaper, see how many times your player can throw a card and get it to land on the newspaper. When your child has used all the cards in the deck, start over, but move the newspaper section a little further away.

Square Mark

Use a newspaper section as a "home base" from which a variety of skills are tried:

- How many lit candles can be extinguished with a water gun?

- How many dominoes can be knocked down with a party blower? (Dominoes can be set up side by side each knocked down one by one, or lined up for a mass knock-down.)

- How far can a spear (newspaper bat, see page **25**) be thrown?

- What is the farthest distance a paper airplane can fly in three trials?

Stepping Stones

Lay some newspaper sections on the floor and pretend they are "stepping stones" that cross a creek. Take turns stepping from one stone to another. You can also take turns moving the stones to form a different pathway. Try putting the stones close together for little steps and then far apart to encourage more of a stretch.

You can also give the child a ball to hold when he

steps from stone to stone asking him to throw it into a basket at the other side of the "creek." Holding a ball with both hands helps little ones learn to use their trunk muscles for better balance and not rely on their outstretched arms.

Agility Run

Lay newspaper sections out in a line, each square a small distance from the last. The players take turns running from the bottom to the top by weaving in and out of the squares like a slalom skier. It's challenging to time each run so that the players work on improving their records. The object is to see how fast you can go without touching the sections.

Variations:

- Bounce a ball while weaving between the sections. Dribbling the ball adds eye-hand coordination to the task. Alternate hands.

- Kick a newspaper ball around sections.

- Have two children go together, one behind the other.

Choo-Choo Slalom

This game is like "Agility Run," except that players get in a line to form a train, which weaves in and out of the squares. The engine of the train has to be sure he leaves enough room for the rest of the train, especially the caboose, to make it around the squares without touching them. What are the squares? They are cows on the track, of course!

Blind Squares

Tape down a "home" section of paper and lay out at least three other sections at different distances and direction from "home." Have your child walk from "home" to each square (name the squares 1, 2, 3, etc.). Then have him close his eyes (or you can use a blindfold or put a paper bag over his head) and walk from home to the square named. For example, say, "You're standing on the 'home' square. I am going to blindfold you and then I want you to walk from here to square #2 and then from there to square #3 and then back to home."

Dizzy Jump

Lay out six or seven newspaper sections in a straight line, then leave a fair amount of space between them and an eighth section. The player jumps from section to section for the first seven sections, then runs around the eighth one at least ten times. When he is properly dizzy, he then attempts to jump the other sections one at a time again.

Throw and Jump

Have your child stand on a stool or chair, according to ability, and hand her a newspaper section. Ask her to throw the paper to the floor and then jump down and land on it. The thicker the section, the more she will be able to control where it lands. This game is best played on a rug so the paper won't slip when she lands on it; if the floor is slippery, you could also tape the paper down after each throw. Then, at the end, there would be a group of taped newspapers at varying distances from each other, and then you could play the next game.

Jumping Difference

Tape newspaper sections down at varying distances from each other so that to jump from one to the other could require a large effort or just a little tiny one. Depending on the accuracy you want to achieve, you could ask the jumper to aim for the center of the paper (mark a large circle in the center for visual aid) or just to touch any part of the paper. The same game, of course, could be done for jumping sideways and backward, leaping, hopping or, for the advanced who still can use work on balance, twirling (turning a full circle in the air before landing).

Broad Jumping

Encourage broad jumping by laying a square down for the child to jump from and having her jump as far as she can. Tape a newspaper down where she lands, and ask her to try again and see whether she can jump further and get past the second newspaper. Next try a running broad jump.

Twirly Squares

Tape a newspaper section to the floor and ask your child to jump in the air and do a quarter turn, a half turn, or a full turn on the square.

Rhythmic Squares

Ask your little one to jump over the square, then to jump forward and immediately jump backward to the starting point. Or have him jump from one side of the square to the other and then back again. You can make up a series of patterns that includes jumping from front to back and then side to side or even on the diagonal. Then, let the child make up a pattern.

Posture Walk

Have children put newspapers on their heads. Encourage the proper posture (straight back, hips tucked under, belly lifted), and go for a stroll!

Newspaper Hats

Remember making hats and boats out of newspapers? Use the illustration for a step-by-step guide to give your child practice in folding and manipulating.

You can also make newspaper hats by taking a single sheet of newspaper and laying it on top of your child's head, putting tape around the crown to keep the paper in place. The excess paper that sticks out beyond the tape can be scrunched up to form the sides of a derby or any other fanciful hat shape.

Tearing Shapes

Using a single sheet of paper, start tearing out simple shapes such as circles and triangle, and go on to more complicated shapes like people and animals.

Ball Flick

Scrunch a small piece of paper into a ball and put masking tape around it to keep it compressed. See how far your player can flick it with a thumb and an index finger.

Have races! Can you and your child flick the balls toward each other and have them crash into each other?

Set up goals, such as two pennies a few inches apart. Can the players flick the ball between two pennies?

A Step at a Time

Scrunch up some newspaper into a ball and wrap it with tape to keep it compressed. Face your child, standing fairly close, and toss the ball back and forth. Every time you successfully catch and throw the ball, take one step back. Continue this game until you or your partner can no longer catch it; then take one step back toward each other. In this way you end the game with success. Remember how many steps you were able to take—"We took ten steps away from each other!"—so that the next time you play you can try for eleven!

For beginners, the same game can be played sitting down and fanny-walking backward after each successful catch. For the very beginning ball player, roll the ball back and forth; but the sophisticated beginning ball player can propel the ball with different parts of his body: elbow, chin, knee, and so on. If necessary, make a larger ball by adding more newspaper.

Have more advanced players put one hand behind their backs and catch with the other.

Upside-Down Roll

Partners turn their backs to each other, bend over from the waist, and toss or roll the newspaper ball back and forth to each other through their legs. (See illustration.) This stance also develops balance and is a good way to get fresh oxygenated blood to the brain!

General Targets

Throw the newspaper ball into or at a variety of targets: a rope coil, a hula hoop, a wastebasket, a dishpan, a bucket, a coffee can, a shoe, a garden hose coil, an inner tube, a bicycle tire, a rock, a street sign, or a hole dug in the ground. Introducing a large variety of targets leads kids into making up their own eye-hand coordinating games.

> *When my two-year-old toddled over to me with her used yogurt container and a small rubber ball and suggested we play a target game with it, I knew she had gotten my message.*

Sheet Targets

Hang up a sheet or one side of a cardboard box with a hole cut in it and ask your child to aim the ball through the hole. Make holes of varying sizes so that there are extremely easy shots as well as difficult ones.

Add a challenging element by standing on the other side of the sheet or cardboard square and tossing the ball back and forth to each other through the hole.

Hula Aims

Hang a hula hoop up and toss the ball back and forth through the hoop with your player. The hoop provides a visual cue to a new ball-thrower as to where to throw the ball.

Living Hoop

Become a human basketball hoop for your child by using your arms to form a large circle, encouraging your player to throw the ball into the "hoop." If you lay down a newspaper for the foul line and then move slowly around the room, you will ensure that your child gets some throws in from her weaker side, as well as giving her

some practice in using her eyes for scanning. Of course, you may sometimes get hit in the face, but then no one said parenting would be free of occupational hazards. To minimize danger, I encourage children to toss gently underhand for this game.

Ball Toss

Using a firmly taped newspaper ball, ask your player to:

- Throw low and catch with two hands

- Throw higher and higher, catching with two hands

- Start low and catch with his dominant hand only

- Catch with his nondominant hand, putting the preferred hand in his pocket or behind his body

- Catch underhand

- Catch overhand

- Throw (low, high), clap once (twice, three times, etc.), before catching with one (two hands)

- Throw the ball against a wall and catch it

- Throw the ball against a wall and clap once and then catch it

- Throw from one hand to another with eyes open and then eyes closed

- Throw underhand and turn around and catch

- Lie down, throw the ball, stand up, and catch it

- Walk and keep ball in the air using just the backs of the hands

- Throw and catch standing on one foot

- Throw and catch with one eye closed (with both eyes closed)

- See how far the player can throw the ball

- Start the ball on her head and catch it with her hands

- Catch the ball in a milk carton, a gallon bottle cut in half with the handle left on, or upside-down traffic cones

Partner Toss

Throw two balls between two people, such as you and your child or your child and a sibling or neighborhood friend, so that both throw and catch at the same time, practically. Vary the rules.

- Both toss underhand.

- Both toss overhand.

- One person tosses underhand and the other overhand.

- One person throws a beat behind the other, or two beats.

- Both balls are thrown by one person, so that the other one has to catch a ball with each hand. (You can have kids gain experience catching with one hand by starting with things that are easy to grasp, such as pillows, scarves, and rag dolls.)

Baseball

Good ole American baseball can be played with newspapers by tightly rolling up and taping a section or two of the paper to form a bat. The thicker the bat, the firmer it is, so construct it with your child's skill level in mind. The ball can also be made larger or smaller depending on how many newspaper sheets you scrunch up.

- Variation: Have the player hold the bat horizontally instead of vertically.

Golf

Golf can be played using the same equipment as baseball, but in a different position, of course. Your "holes" can be taped newspaper squares, with the object being to see how many strokes it takes to get from one square to another.

Croquet

Use a newspaper ball and bats, and lay down some cardboard boxes for wickets. The boxes should be open at either end.

Badminton

Use real badminton racquets, a newspaper ball for a birdie, and a hanging hula hoop for a net. This is not exactly regulation equipment, but it'll work. Balloons make nice birdies too.

Soccer

Have your child "dribble" a newspaper ball with a foot as players do in soccer. Dribbling involves moving the ball along the ground in a controlled fashion while walking or running. The ball should be tapped gently with the inside or outside of the foot and should never be more than one foot ahead of the "dribbler." It is stopped with the sole of the foot. Once your child gets the idea, make up a slalom course with newspaper squares around which the ball is to be maneuvered.

Aimed Kicking

Set up a group of chairs and ask the kicker to aim her ball through the legs of the different chairs. Or tape a picture on a wall and have the child kick the ball at the target. A box lying on its side makes another good target.

Partner Kicking

Kick the newspaper ball back and forth to each other.

Hackeysak Ball

Put the newspaper ball on your foot and toss to yourself or others using only feet and knees to keep it off the floor.

Kicking

How far can your players kick a newspaper ball with first the right leg and then the left? Can they kick it farther each time? How about kicking it back and forth to each other?

Stair Toss

Throw a flattened newspaper ball on different steps of a staircase. A reward like raisins, nuts, or fruit could be placed on each step for added incentive, with the child allowed to eat whatever is on the step the ball lands on. The child might want to call out the number of the step she is trying for.

Blind Walk

Scrunch up newspaper to form a ball and place it a distance away. Ask your player to close her eyes or wear a blindfold, then walk to where the paper is laid and pick it up. This is harder than it sounds. Try it yourself when it's your turn.

Kangaroo Ball

Place a newspaper ball on the ground and ask your player to pick it up with his knees and jump around like a kangaroo—slow jumps, long jumps, sideways jumps. If you or others are playing you could add bumping into each other (hip to hip), trying to dislodge the balls.

Ball Dance

Ask your child to move a ball around her waist, first in one direction, then in the other. Next have her move it around one knee, then the other knee, then both of them. Get her to do a figure eight, or go around a thigh with the other leg lifted.

The Plow

Players lie on their backs, arms out to the sides. Put a large newspaper ball behind their heads and encourage them to stretch their legs over their heads to pick up the ball. (The Plow is a Yoga position.)

Bat Balance #1

Newspaper bats are easy to make: Simply roll up a section of newspaper and tape it tightly. Balance a newspaper bat horizontally on her hand, her fingers, her thumb, and on one finger. Can she walk while balancing the newspaper bat? Now have her try the other hand. How about her knee, her elbow . . .

Bat Balance #2

Have your child balance the bat vertically on his open palm, finger, arm, foot, chin, nose . . .

Bat Toss

Suggest that your child:

- Toss the bat up and catch it

- Toss the bat up and give it a half spin and catch the other end

- Toss the bat back and forth from hand to hand

- Twirl the bat like a baton, winding it around his body and under his legs, making a figure eight

Quicker Than the Eye

In this game the child holds a bat out horizontally in front of her with one hand, then releases it and catches with the other. Have her try the same thing holding the bat vertically. This game encourages fast reflexes.

So how fast are your child's reflexes? Hold the bat vertically above her head. On the count of three, drop it and see how fast she can catch it.

Mark the spot where your player caught it the first time and see whether she can catch it more quickly the next time.

Have her try each hand and see whether there is a difference between the reflexes of the two sides.

Sword Fights

The newspaper bats seem to elicit this game with everyone, whether I want them to or not. The game is a definite winner for tension reducing and general laughs. In this one, you and your child take a bat and "en garde" and "touché" each other until the bats bend.

Bat Jump

Lay a bat down on the floor and have your player jump back and forth over it. Go back and forth slowly and then quickly. Go back and forth with a certain rhythm, such as two jumps in place on each side before jumping over. Jump around the bat forward and backward.

Bat Walk

If you've played a lot of games with your newspaper bats and they are looking pretty wilted, get one more game out of them by laying them down end to end and asking your players to walk on them like a tightrope. Unlike a regular tightrope, however, you can make yours have all sorts of angles that encourage watching where one's feet are going!

Staying Loose

The player holds a newspaper bat in both hands in front of her body and parallel to the floor, then steps over the bat with each foot until it is behind her body; then, she steps back over until the bat is in its original position.

Magic Wand

In this activity, the children stand in a line in front of you as you hold a magic wand. (The wand looks suspiciously like a rolled-up newspaper bat to those who don't believe in magic.) Explain that you are going to swing the wand horizontally and try to touch everyone's head and turn them into frogs. Whoever doesn't want to become a frog should duck, so to speak. You might also swing the wand to touch their feet, in order to turn them into donkeys. Those not in the mood to be a donkey must jump over the wand.

Swing at the players' heads and feet in random order, giving players a split second to jump or duck. Those who are touched by the magic wand must leave the circle and make "ribbit" or "hee-haw" noises, depending on what they were turned into. The game ends when all the players have been transformed into frogs or donkeys. (Magic works!)

Magic Changes

The group sits in a circle with the newspaper bat in the center and chants, "A bat, a bat, what else can it be . . .?" or "Magic, Magic, Magic Do/What else can this be to you?"

One player picks up the bat and uses it like a back scratcher.

The group then chants the same words and the next person picks up the bat and uses it in another way—a magic wand, pogo stick, saxophone, stick horse, oars, snorkel, drum major baton, cane, pole vaulter, barbells, guitar. Anything is possible.

The chanting in between each turn gives the next player an extra moment to plan something. A short song could be used instead of a chant, or a chant could be done in sign language.

You could use a newspaper section for another round. What else could it be? A giant washrag, you say. Well then, let everyone take a pretend shower and try it out!

GROUP NEWSPAPER GAMES

If you are playing with kids of different ages and skill levels, these newspaper games work well. As each child goes from square to square using the method of

locomotion that you call out, you can tailor your instruction to the child's abilities. You might ask the obviously well coordinated child to do complicated procedures like twirling or doing a Ninja Turtle karate kick with each movement, and ask the younger child simply to jump or to do some of the other less complicated movements, like jumping sideways and backward.

Lily Pads

Lay down newspaper squares on the floor so that each child has his or her own. Explain to the group that these are not really newspaper squares but lily pads, and that they aren't really kids, they are frogs! (Of course—silly them.) Have each frog stand on a lily pad while you put on music or sing a song. While the music is happening, the frogs have to jump around, frog-like, until the music stops—at which point they have to race madly to a pad. You will have removed one pad each time, of course, but in this game it doesn't mean the padless player is out; he or she has to share a pad with another frog. When the music starts up again, you can suggest different ways they must move each time: skipping, walking backward, hopping, etc. They will finally get to the point where quite a lot of them are squeezing together on one pad. The only rule is that some part of each frog's body has to touch the square. It's okay if someone is holding on to or even lifting up another frog. This game encourages physical

closeness, which has a way of making kids feel friendlier toward each other. After all, they are all in the same dilemma of having to get part of their body on the pad.

Circle Squares

The players stand in a circle, with everyone on his or her own section of newspaper. From here they can:

- Take hands and slowly lower themselves as a group to squatting, then go from there back to standing.

- Join hands and start to sway from side to side. In this activity, everyone becomes aware of everyone else, so that eventually the whole circle is swaying together. They'll know when it is not quite right and when they are perfectly in sync.

- Stay in rhythm with each other and jump from one section to the other in the circle. One person jumps off her section just as the next person jumps onto it. Establishing a rhythm with a drum or a song helps people get in sync with each other.

Variations: Jump sideways or backward; enlarge the spaces between the squares. If the players are agile and

the sections don't slip, try jumping while doing a full turn in the air before landing on the next section.

Square Races

Have children put a newspaper square on their heads and see how fast they can race.

Relay Squares

A relay game can be done with newspaper squares. Put one square down to mark Point A, the starting point, and another to mark point B, the goal. Each team of three should have its own set of squares so that no player has to wait too long for a turn.

HOW one gets from point A to point B is up for grabs. Here are some possibilities.

- Run to the other square, hop around it, and run back.

- Walk backward to the other square, skip around it backward, and run back.

- Skip to the other square, jump over it, and hop back.

- Gallop to the other square, stand on it and sing out your name, and march back.

- Bear-walk to the other square, stand on it and touch your nose to your toes, and twirl back. (Bear-walking is like crawling except that you extend your legs and walk on flat feet.)

- Walk sideways to the square, tiptoe around it, and then crawl home backward.

Player could take turns making the rules.

How close or far apart point A and B are depends on the skill level and "antsyness" factor of your group. The longer the run, the more energy it takes, and the longer people have to wait their turn.

This isn't a competition. Each team gets points if everyone on the team finishes—somewhere between fifty and a zillion points or thereabouts.

Everyone wins!

Shocking Squares

Lay out a random pattern of newspaper sections in a specified area. The players have to move within this space without touching the squares, which you could declare to be electrified and deadly. It's fun to use music to set the tone and speed. If someone touches a square and falls down dead, she has to lie still and becomes a new

obstacle, also dangerously shocking. Whoever is left standing gets to lay out the squares for the next game. To add even more challenge at different times in the game, reduce the space of the specified area. A flexible garden hose or rope could be used and could be adjusted for a smaller and smaller circle.

To add variety, change the way players have to move in that space. Hop? Skip? Jump? Jump sideways? Backward?

Private Squares

In this game each player stands on a section of newspaper and follows the instructions you call out. Everyone is so involved in her own movements that children who are shy, have special needs, or are younger feel freer to be more internal and less self-conscious.

Possible instructions are:

- "Stand on your own square and do something beautiful (or silly, mean, dumb, happy, strict, etc.)."

- "Stand like a sleeping stork, one leg up."

- "Skip around your square."

- "Stand on one foot and then switch feet. How many ways can you switch feet?"

- "Jump over your square from front to back (or from side to side or diagonally)."

- "Straddle the square, then jump on top of it; reverse."

- "Go around the square sideways, facing it. Do the same with your back to the square. Now switch from front to back as you go around."

- "Touch the square with only an elbow and a knee (or ulnar and patella bone, if you are teaching anatomy)."

- "Make a dance: For example, two jumps on the square, one forward and one back, and a hop to either side." (Each player could choreograph his own pattern and shows it to the group.)

Notice the different ways the children do these movements and, if it seems appropriate, point these out to the others. "Roxanne has an interesting way of doing that. Let's all do it like her." You could also give an open-ended task: "Move on your section any way that you want." Then comment, "Let's all try Marissa's way" or "Let's all copy Peter's idea."

Trusting Squares

Two players stand on their own newspaper sections across from each other, their palms facing forward and

touching. Their sections are far enough apart that the players have to lean slightly forward.

The game is to push off with their hands and then fall forward again, catching each other with their outstretched palms. The braver players can catch each other with their arms.

The farther apart the squares, the trickier the game is. And then, of course, there is the variation of doing it with the eyes closed . . .

Carrying Game

Lay newspaper sections down in a circle or in a path. Each section is occupied by one person except for one, which has two people on it. One of these two carries the other to the next section, where the person who was carried now carries the next person to the next section, and so on, until everyone has had a turn carrying or being carried.

If a smaller person has to carry a larger person, the carrier may be able to carry only one leg, meaning that the person being "carried" has to do some hopping.

Variation: Have two people on each section with three on the first. In this version the two people doing the carrying have to form a seat with their arms to carry the third person.

Line Pitching

In this fast-moving ball game, children line up behind each other facing a pitcher. The pitcher throws the ball to the catcher at the front of the line. The catcher catches the ball and then changes place with the pitcher and gets ready to toss the ball to the next kid in line; the former pitcher goes to the end of the line. It takes a moment for everyone to get used to who goes where, when, but when they do, this game runs like a smooth machine, giving every player the chance to catch and throw, with practically no waiting time between turns.

Line Crawling

This is another line ball game, except that in this one the children pass the ball from the front of the line to the rear, over their heads, to the players behind them. The person at the end of the line then crawls on hands and knees through the legs of the other children until she reaches the front of the line, at which time the ball passing begins again. The game ends when the last person crawls through.

You can add to the excitement of this game by asking the players to begin by standing with their legs wide apart. Then, with each successive crawler, have

them narrow their stance until the last crawlers have to squeeze through the legs by turning their bodies sideways.

Color Toss

Stand in a circle and have the players toss the ball to the person who has yellow on, or blue, or whatever color you call out. You can also say things like "blue eyes" or "brown hair" to increase awareness of personal differences.

Running the Gauntlet

In this game, two lines of players face each other, leaving about ten feet between them. Each player is armed with a newspaper ball. Four or five other players then stand on one end of this gauntlet, ready to run between this double file of children. In order to prevent the game from turning into a wild free-for-all, tell the players that it only counts if they hit the runners on their backs, for example. Every runner hit on the back then joins one side or the other of the two lines. For the next run-through with the remaining players, tell the gauntleteers they must hit the

back of the legs, the hands, the shoulders, or whatever. Once all the runners have been hit, a new group of runners is formed. Scrunched-up newspaper balls taped lightly don't hurt when you get hit by them, so runners get the thrill of the adrenaline rush without the pain.

Pattern Ball

If you have a small group, have the players toss the newspaper ball to each other and then remember the pattern so they can repeat it. For example, first Joe threw the ball to Sally, who threw the ball to Eric, who then threw the ball to Jennifer, and so on. Everybody has to remember the sequence as you switch objects to throw. Find unusual things to throw, such as scarves, can lids, rolled up socks . . .

Circle Ball Games

Have the children stand in a circle and throw newspaper balls to each other, but keep calling out variations:

- Throw the ball to the person beside you

- Throw the ball to the person across from you

- Throw the ball to someone who has red on

- Throw the ball to someone whose name starts with the letter *(whatever)*

- Throw the ball to someone with blue (green, brown, gold) eyes; brown (blonde, red, black) hair; short (long, medium) hair

- Name the person you are going to throw to

Vary the size of the ball by adding more scrunched up sheets of paper; the more tape you add, the firmer the ball.

Wastebasketball

This is like "Living Hoop" on page 22, except this time the hoop is a child standing on a chair with a wastebasket. The idea is that the child can move the basket in the direction of the shot to help teammates make a basket. I've know some kids who will move the basket away at the very last second, making their pals lose a shot, but that's another kind of game.

Human Pinball

Children form a circle facing outward with one person is in the center. That player bends over and shoots the

newspaper ball through his legs at someone's back. The one hit becomes "It" and moves to the center of the circle, and the process is repeated.

Cross-Over Dodgeball

Form two lines of players facing each other. The children throw balls at players in the other line. When players are hit, they cross over to the other team.

One section of newspaper makes a soft ball that doesn't hurt. Still, if there is any problem with people throwing the ball too hard, increase the distance between the two lines.

Group Hurdles

In this game children kneel in a line, holding newspaper bats out in front. The last person in the line gets up and jumps over all the hurdles before taking his place in front, when the last person in line begins. You might want to have someone say how high the bat hurdles are held.

Number Bats

If you have a slew of bats made, divide the group up into smaller groups and have each group take the bats and form a number between one and ten with them. Then the whole class has to jump, hop, skip, bunny hop, crab walk, or just slouch along that number of times. Each group decides the movement that will accompany its number.

Bat Relay

Two teams line up side by side. The first player runs, touches an agreed-upon goal with a bat, runs back, and hands the bat to the next player in line.

Swat Tag

This is a more grown-up version of "Duck, Duck, Goose" using newspaper bats. The players are seated in a circle. Player #1 touches everyone's back as she walks around the circle until she strikes one more firmly, at which point she runs around the circle with the "strikee" in pursuit. The idea is for the striker to try and put the bat in a box in the middle of the circle and sit in the "strikee's" vacant spot before getting tagged.

CHAPTER THREE

Games to play with milk, yogurt and ice cream containers

IF YOU ARE PART of a milk-drinking family, half-gallon milk cartons seem to be the one item that accumulate quickly, which is fortunate, as they work well for games. (Games with plastic gallon containers are listed under chapter 12, "Games to Play with Other Things") Yogurt and pint ice cream containers and their lids are useful too. And if people ask you why you are suddenly downing pints of Ben & Jerry's Super Chocolate Fudge Brownie ice cream, you can righteously reply that you are doing it for your children.

Giant Dice Jump

Cut the tops off two milk cartons, leaving about three quarters of the carton intact, and fit one carton bottom into the other to make a cube. Cover the cube with butcher or any white paper and mark it like dice: one dot on one side, two dots on another, etc.

Make a list of motor activities, such as jumping, hopping, skipping, leaping, turning, and sliding.

Then have each child choose an activity and throw the dice to find out how many times to do that activity.

Milk Carton Blocks

Make blocks the same way you did the dice by cutting the tops off of milk cartons and fitting the ends inside each other. Make them different sizes by varying how big an end you cut off.

Use these blocks for building walls and towers. Have one child do it all, or take turns, with children adding a block at a time to the construction. When it's all done, everyone gets to kick it down. Of course, the hard part for kids is waiting till the last carton is on before kicking it down. Anticipation elicits excitement, and excitement makes little legs itchy, and sometimes the tower gets kicked prematurely. Oh, well!

The more blocks you have, the bigger the tower or wall and the greater the challenge, meaning that with enough blocks, even older kids enjoy this one, especially when it gets to the point where one has to stand on a chair or stepladder to add the next block. And no matter what the age, there seems to be a thrill in making it "all fall down!"

Children can also knock down the milk carton structure using a bean bag or ball or anything else handy, including another milk carton block.

If you want, you can make the blocks prettier and last longer by covering them with contact or wrapping paper. I've done this, but to tell you the truth, I find that prettier milk cartons only serve to impress other adults, while the kids really don't care. Once I covered cartons with extra butcher paper and drew lovely little designs on them. I had fun drawing the designs, but I found that when the kids started playing rough with the cartons, standing on them, kicking them, and all the other things I wanted them to do, it bothered me. I hated to see my pretty things get dirty! Useless attitude. I don't cover them any more. I let the kids squash and kick them to their hearts' content and it doesn't bother me a bit.

Progressive Jumps

The players start off jumping over one carton lying on its side. Another block is added so that they are jumping over two, then another, and another, until the jump is beyond the outer limits of everyone's jumping skills.

Then ask them to stand back a ways from the cartons to get a good running start and try leaping over the stack.

Slots

Make a milk carton block as described above and cut a slot in the top as if it were a piggy bank. Then take a side of a carton and cut strips narrow enough to fit into the slots. Make them about half an inch long as longer strips tend to bend.

Have your player put the strips into the slot. Variations:

- Cut strips of different widths and make slots of coordinating widths for the child who is ready to see size variations.

- Make circles instead of slots and use marbles or small beads. If the worker is still mouthing things and is likely to put marbles and beads in her mouth, use large objects like walnuts and corks instead.

Milk Carton Houses

Cut doors and windows in a milk carton. If you use two cartons, tape them together. Then paint the house with thick tempera paint. Children can move miniature people and toys through the different doors and windows, making up a story to go along with the movements.

Milk Carton Squish

Instead of having a path of milk cartons that children jump over, make a path of cartons that children can jump on!

Jumping with full force and squashing one carton after another will satisfy the hearts of many a young child.

Squished Carton Throw

No use in wasting a perfectly good squished carton from the game of **Milk Carton Squish** (described above) when it can be used to play a how-far-can-you-throw-it game. Mark a line and have each player take a turn throwing his carton. Or make a longer line and let everyone throw at once. (One, two, three, THROW!) Or do it both ways.

Or point out a target. Outside it might be a tree; inside it could be a spot on the wall. Let the kids see how accurately they can aim their throws.

Carton Drop

Open up the spout or entire top of an empty milk carton and have children stand above it dropping objects into it. Objects can vary depending on what's readily available. What about pebbles? Chalk? Pencils? Erasers?

The height from which objects are dropped can vary as well. Have players try sitting on a chair. How about standing on a desk? Standing on a stepladder?

It might be interesting for children to give themselves ten tries at each different height and make a chart on the differences in their scores.

Circles in Squares

Cut up the sides of milk cartons to get flat rectangles. Cut these in half and cut a large hole in the center of each square. Now, using a paper towel tube have your learner place the square on the tube. (You can sit the tube upright by cutting a hole in another carton or in a cereal box.) As your child gets more proficient, make the holes smaller and use a dowel or cut-up broomstick handle instead of a paper towel tube.

Carton Ring Toss

Milk carton rings can be made by slicing milk cartons the way you would slice a pound cake. The rings can then tossed over any upright object, such as a plastic shampoo bottle filled with water.

Jump in the Spaces

Stand milk cartons in a row, allowing plenty of space between them. The game is to jump over each carton until you get to the end of the line. Jump sideways and backward, too. Then hop over each carton on one foot.

Wide-Legged Jump

This is a good one for beginning jumpers who haven't the coordination yet to jump over the cartons but can do a sort of slide and shuffle jump beside them. It gives them a sense of jumping and requires them to notice where their feet are in relation to the cartons.

Lay the cartons out in a long row and have the player use a wide-gait position to jump down the row, the cartons between his feet.

Jumping Blocks

Glue four to eight milk cartons together to form a block and cover them with contact paper or tape to make sure they stay together. Use several of these blocks in obstacle courses to be jumped, crawled, or leaped over, depending on the age and skill level of your players.

Walking Maze

Make a maze out of the cartons and have the player walk through it several times with eyes open. Then have her try it with eyes shut and see whether she can build an internal map of where the cartons are.

Arrows

Cut out small arrows from the sides of milk cartons. You can get one or two arrows out of each side of a carton.

The smaller the child, the larger the arrow. Give three or more to your learner and the same number to yourself. Make a pattern with your arrows. For example, in a line of three arrows, the two outer ones could point to each other and the middle one could point up. Ask your learner to make her arrows look exactly like yours.

If this task is too easy, show her your pattern, cover it with a scarf, and ask her to do it from memory. If it is too difficult, ask your player to put her arrows on top of yours.

The more arrows you use and the more varied the pattern, the greater the challenge.

Line 'em Up!

Cut the tops off some cartons and stand them in a row facing the player, who tests his aim by trying to throw a small hard object such as a walnut or cork into one of the cartons.

You can increase the chances of success by clustering a few cartons together instead of lining them up single file. Or, for greater challenge, line the cartons up and number them 1, 2, 3, etc. Then ask the player to call out the number of the carton he's aiming for. Can he make his target? How about from farther away?

Walk and Kick

Line up a row of cartons and then have the player walk along and kick them down one by one.

Milk Carton Soccer

Using the milk carton like a ball, kick the carton from one end of the room to the other. Use two standing cartons, slightly separated, to be the goal posts. Or make more than one set of goal posts around the room. Arrange some goal posts to be wider and therefore easier to get through, and others to be narrower and more challenging.

Variation: Use any kind of container to make a series of goals at which the players can aim. The children must "dribble" the carton from one goal to the next, hitting each container in turn or going around it. (See illustration.)

This game can be played by one person or by a group divided into two teams, with goals on each end of the "field."

Kick Around

Set up a row of milk cartons about a foot apart and then have the player kick a yogurt container around the cartons in a slalom fashion from one end of the line to the other.

Hop Around

Set up two parallel rows of four milk cartons each. Have the players hop in a circle around each carton, going from one to another. If the rows are close together, it takes tighter control to hop around one without knocking another one down. If they are very far apart, then it takes more strength and endurance to go from one row to another.

Milk Carton Path

Set up two parallel rows of milk cartons as in "Hop Around," but this time lay the cartons on their sides and have the player walk on them, stepping from one to the other. The fact that they squish or jiggle when walking on them adds to the balancing challenge.

Milk Carton Tower Path

This is like "Milk Carton Path," except that cartons are placed upright. The cartons tend to squish and jiggle even more in this position, so your player might need a steadying hand or supporting arm.

Shoe Shuffle

Turn cartons into shoes for small feet by cutting out one of the sides. See how fast your player can move in these shoes; or make him a path to follow.

Balancing Walk

A variation on the ever-faithful balancing-a-book-on-your-head exercise: How many milk cartons can your child balance on her head ? Start with one and add on while the player is standing still.

Then start again with one carton and see how far the player can get while walking. Can she get that far balancing two cartons?

Milk Carton Balance

If you stuff milk cartons with newspapers as tightly as you can, they make a box sturdy enough to stand on. Start with two on the floor and have players stand on them. Then add two more to form a second layer, placing them crossways to the first two to make a sturdier foundation. Add as many more layers as skill level allows.

Milk Carton Jump

Stand milk cartons in a row like a miniature wall facing the player. Ask him to run and leap over them or stand in front of them and jump over them. Keep adding more cartons to the wall to increase its height.

Milk Carton Leap

This time, lay the milk cartons down end to end in a long line and invite players to leap over it. Start with just a few cartons and then keep adding more, increasing the length of the line.

Milk Carton Percussion Sounds

Cut off the tops of milk cartons and fit them together in pairs as before. You can make different-sized blocks by varying the height at which you cut off the tops, or by using smaller containers such as pints or half-pints.

Instead of using these blocks for building, however, put different things inside each one—things like stones, pennies, bells, popcorn, bottle caps, buttons, gravel, beans, rice, salt, sand, etc. Ask your player to identify the objects inside of each block by sound as you gently shake each carton. Or, make two of each kind of sound block and ask your listener to find the ones that match.

Use the different sounds of these blocks to make music. For beginners, demonstrate loud sounds and soft sounds by varying the force and speed of the shaking.

Ask older players to imagine what animal their block sound reminds them of. Maybe the one filled with pennies makes them think of birds, while the one with stones sounds more like elephants. Ask each player to make up a rhythmic shaking of the blocks to go with the animal idea. Birds might inspire a 2:4 rhythm and elephants a 1:2 beat.

Some children might be inspired to "write" their own music making a score that reads: "Cube 2—shake 2 times. Cube 1—four times. Cube 6—1 time," and so on.

Throw the Dice

Make the dice suggested in "Giant Dice Jump (page 50).

Seat the players in a circle; each takes a turn throwing the dice to see who gets the highest number. Except that instead of rolling these dice, the children toss them up in the air, giving them a spin, if they are able, and let them fall in the center of the circle.

Vary the rules so that the person with the lowest number wins, or the person who throws even (or odd) numbers win.

Another way to play is to give the children three turns each and then have them add up their scores. The highest (or lowest) score wins! A painless way to practice addition skills.

Hot Box

This is a game of "keep-away." Certain people in the group are the throwers and others are the "interceptors." The throwers make a circle around the interceptors and throw the milk carton to other throwers. The person who successfully intercepts a throw then changes places with that thrower.

Drop Box

This game calls for paying attention. Everyone in the group is given a milk carton. One person is designated ahead of each game as the dropper; when this person drops her carton, the others immediately have to drop theirs. The first person to catch on to what's happening, and drop his carton, can be the dropper for the next drop.

Soccer

Children play a regular game of soccer, with one team trying to kick the carton from one side of the room to the other, while the others are trying to get it to go in the opposite direction. You can place two cartons on each side of the room to mark the goals.

Bat the Carton

Kelvin and Tyler from my movement class came up with this game, one in which two people bat the carton back and forth with their hands as if it were a volleyball. As the boys got more confident, they elaborated on the rules to say that each person had to bat the carton twice to himself before batting it to the other person.

Milk Carton Fence

If you have a large number of milk carton blocks at your disposal, ask the children to build a common wall, making it as wide and tall as possible. If you wish, have each child take a turn adding to the wall. When you say, "go," everyone gets to run at the wall and knock it down (the fun part).

Mountain Jumps

Place one carton or a pile of cartons in the middle of the room, and have the players run and jump over them as if the cartons were a huge mountain and they were huger giants.

It's really satisfying to have the other players yell out the jumper's name just as she is clearing the mountain top!

PLASTIC CONTAINER GAMES

Match the Lid

If you have a variety of different kinds of yogurt and ice cream containers, you can have your player find the right lid to go on the right container, providing practice in putting things on and taking them off, as well as the cognitive skill of matching.

Yogurt Toss #1

Use one yogurt container and a hard object, such as an eraser or a walnut, and have the player toss the object into the air and catch it with the yogurt container. Start tossing a small object, and encourage the player to toss it higher and higher.

Yogurt Toss #2

Use two yogurt containers (or cut the tops off two milk cartons or use ice cream pint containers), and have the player toss a small hard object from one container to the next. Again, the higher the toss, the greater the challenge.

Two-Hand Toss

Have the child toss a small yogurt container (with the lid on) from one hand to the other until she is confident enough to toss two containers from hand to hand at the same time.

If you know how to teach juggling, add a third container to the repertoire. Yogurt containers won't roll away as easily as balls, although I find scarves and other materials are even easier for first-time jugglers.

Frisbee Knock-Down

This game requires empty yogurt and ice cream containers and their lids. Place the containers on the floor, upside down. Then have the player sit, stand, or squat a certain distance away and use the lids like frisbees to hit the containers.

The containers can be in a line or in a random pattern, the closer ones being easier to hit and the ones farther away requiring more force.

Block the Container

Annie, another student in one of my movement classes, thought of this one. Two people stand facing each other holding hands, while the others line up as if everyone were about to play a game of "London Bridges," except the players in line are holding ice cream containers and are trying to throw them over or under the "bridge" (connected arms), while the two people forming the bridge try and block the container. The game moved along well and was in a nice range of not too difficult and not too easy.

Yogurt Tower

One day I was doing a workshop for a community college class using yogurt containers, lids, and walnuts. We had been throwing, catching, jumping, hopping, running, singing, and pretending for almost two hours, and as we sat, exhausted, in a goodbye circle, I asked whether anyone could come up with one more new game.

Gail, an artist, put a container upside down in the middle of the circle and challenged the rest of us to add a container or a lid, one at a time, and build a tower that wouldn't fall over. We went around the circle, each person adding something to the increasingly precarious tower, and each time the tower got higher and still stayed stable, we collectively sighed in appreciation. I was pleased that when someone finally put on the container that caused the tower to topple, everyone spontaneously clapped and laughed, reflecting the fact that keeping the tower up was a group effort, not one individual's responsibility.

Another advantage of this game is that it can be played by a group of people with a wide variety of skill levels, or when everyone is too tired to move but still up for playing just one more game.

Games to play with garden hose and plumbing pipe

YOU MAY NOT HAVE considered garden hose to be a good source of creative play ideas for your children, but if you try the ideas in this chapter, you'll be in for a pleasant surprise!

Homemade Hula Hoops

Make your own hula hoops by getting some black plastic three-quarter-inch PVC pipe from any building supply store. Cut off sections that are about eight or nine feet long. Using a three-quarter-inch plastic coupling or a piece of doweling, form them into circles.

A ten- or eleven-foot length makes a gigantic circle for running through. (See "Round Runner," on page 84.)

Rings

Make small hoops to use for a variety of games by taking small sections of flexible garden hose—ten to fifteen inches—and making circles. Connect them with appropriate-size doweling.

HOOP GAMES
Hoop Movements

The hoops can be laid down in a variety of patterns, with each pattern inspiring a different set of movements.

For example:

- In the first illustration, where the hoops are in a circle, the players could jump or hop in each circle or alternate between jumping in one and hopping in the next. Or . . .

- . . . They could do a different movement in each circle, like twirl, jump backward, hop, or jump sideways.

- When the hoops are laid in the form of a square, as in the second illustration, the players could be encouraged to jump sideways and backward and to make one-quarter pivot turns before each jump as they change direction.

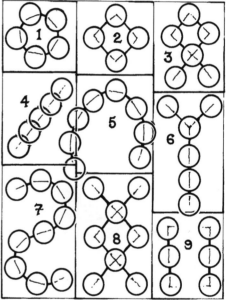

- The third layout is like a hopscotch pattern. Have the players jump in the double hoops and hop in the single ones, both forward and backward. This is also a good pattern for encouraging youngsters to make up their own movements.

- In the fourth illustration, players tiptoe from one small space to another or hop in the large space and tiptoe in the small. For an added challenge, try it sideways with a cross-over step.

These are just some of the possibilities for you to try. You and your players will be bound to come up with many more.

Leaping Lizards

The hoops are laid out in a straight line, with one hoop at the end of the line separated from the others by a few feet. How far apart the hoops are depends on the size of the leapers, because the idea is for the players to see how fast they can leap from one hoop, to the next, run around the last hoop and run back home. The next player begins when the player before is a few hoops ahead. Remind your players that to "run back home" means to run BESIDE the hoops back to the start. If the player ran back ON the hoops while the next player was jumping toward the end hoop, there would be a sorry crash of bodies.

For extra fun, invite the players to pretend they are lizards leaping from rock to rock, frogs jumping from lily pad to lily pad, or whatever else they'd like to be!

Eggbeater Hoop

Spin a hoop on its edge like an eggbeater, and see how many times it is possible to run around it before it stops spinning.

74

Hoop Variety

Lay out a series of hoops and put a different movement activity in each one: a bell, a jump rope, a ball, two bean bags, and so on. How the equipment is used each time could vary. The first round could be to ring the bell twice, jump rope three times, bounce the ball four times, and throw the two bean bags in the air at the same time and catch them (or at least try). On the second round the instructions could remain the same, with the activity timed on both rounds to see whether it can be done faster the second time; or new instructions could be given for each piece of equipment.

Jumping Rope Hoop

Hoops can be used jump rope-style. Have the player hold one part of the hoop and place the rest behind him. He then swings the hoop over his head; and when it gets to the feet, he jumps over it, continuing in a rhythmic pattern. Once players master this skill, have them try jumping backward, or jumping while moving.

Hoop Ball

Have one person hold a hoop while two others throw a ball back and forth to each other through the hoop.

This is a good game for beginning throwers because it gives them visual clues as to where to aim the ball.

If you want to get a little fancier, have the hoop holder move the hoop up and down, thus adding the element of timing and rhythm.

Variations:

- Hang the hoop and then twirl or swing it just as the player gets ready to throw. Talk about timing . . .

- One person holds the hoop on the ground, and the other players bounce the ball through the hoop to each other. As the hoop holder gradually raises the hoop, the other players have to adjust their bounces by varying the distance or the strength with which they bounce the ball.

Hoop Batter

Hang a hoop from a tree limb or a clothes line, or have someone hold the hoop in the air between the thrower and batter. (See illustration.) An inflated balloon is tossed through the hoop to the batter, who bats it back though the hoop with a newspaper bat (sheets of newspaper rolled lengthwise and taped tightly). Playing baseball with a balloon is a guaranteed winner for beginners.

Badminton Hoop

Use badminton rackets and a birdie, but play the game with a hoop instead of a net.

Ring People Toss

Children take turns being poles while the thrower tosses the large hula hoops over their taut bodies. The children who are being the poles can protect their faces by turning their backs to the thrower (this position also adds an element of surprise) or by covering their faces with their hands. They can also extend their height by putting their arms together stiffly overhead.

Because players take turns being poles, they learn to throw gently at their partner. They are the pole next.

If your group is a little too rough or uncoordinated for this game, check out the next one.

Ring Chair Toss

This is just like "Ring People Toss" except that you ring chairs instead of people.

Hoop Croquet

Use a newspaper bat as a croquet mallet, a balloon as a ball, and hoops as wickets. If you can't figure out a way to get the hoops to stand up (see illustration for ideas), use them lying down. Then the idea will be to get the balloon *into* the hoop, rather than *through* it, before you go on to the next wicket.

This game can also be played more like golf. Get a good distance between the starting point and the hoop, and see how many times you have to "drive" the balloon with the "club" before it makes it into the "hole" (hoop).

Hoop Toss

Toss a hoop up and catch it, using both hands. Try one hand. Make it twirl in the air when it's tossed. Try and ring an arm for a catch. Try to ring a leg.

Take a Hoop Walk

In the spirit of the nineties (1890s, that is), show children how to take the hoop for a walk by rolling it along beside them with a stick.

Hanging Hoop

Hang a hoop from a tree limb or ceiling hook and have your learner fly paper airplanes through it.

Hoop Kick

This is my personal favorite. Roll a hoop toward the kicker, who stands sideways in relation to the oncoming hoop. As it nears, the player kicks the side of the hoop with the side of her foot; if this is done correctly (and it doesn't take much practice to get it right), the hoop will fly up in the air, and the person who rolled it should easily be able to catch it. This is great fun for everyone!

Moving Circle Hoop

This game requires music—either live or recorded. Have children join hands to form a circle, with two children joining hands through a large hoop. When the music starts, players begin to step through the hoop to the left, one by one. The object is to see how many times the team can get the hoop around the circle (or move the circle of players through the hoop) before the music stops.

Variation: Use more than one hoop for each circle. How many more than one hoop? Let your sense of fun and the skill level of the players guide your decision.

Tiptoe Hoop Maze

Lay a bunch of hoops on the ground so that they are overlapping each other. Players have to tiptoe in the open spaces from one to the other without stepping on the hoops. (See illustration.) The more hoops used, the more difficult the task.

Have two or more people hold hands or waists and tiptoe through the space. The more people go at the same time, the trickier the walk.

Broad Jump Hoop

Lay a hoop on the ground and ask your player to jump over the whole hoop in a broad-jump style. This game is obviously for the longer-legged group. As a variation, lay out a line of hoops for a series of broad jumps, making sure to leave sufficient space in between for landing.

Race Car Hoops

Players hold the hoops like steering wheels; rev up and start zooming! The idea is to go as fast as possible without crashing into another car.

The smaller the space, the more the players learn the necessity of finding the empty spaces to move into.

Note: Telling the children, "Don't bang into other cars" seems to invite trouble. Children often don't hear the "Don't" part of the sentence; that word just serves to get their attention. What they hear is, "Bang into other cars"! If you say instead, "Go into the empty spaces," it gives them a definite positive suggestion.

Players can hook up with other players by flipping their hoops over the person in front of them and forming a line. The front person holds the hoop flat like a steering wheel of a bus. Everyone stays together and goes for a drive.

Tunnel Walk

Hold hoops up on their sides and have children walk
through them as if through a tunnel. The game is especially good for toddlers, who are discovering how big
they are and what they can fit through. Hoop holders can
be willing adults or other children.

Figure Eight

Lay two hoops out at a slight distance from each other
and show players how to go around them in a figure
eight pattern. This is hard for little ones just learning a
spatial sense, but a good way to help them learn.

If they are getting good at it or are older, add extra
challenges like: How fast can you do it? Can you do it
running backward? Can you do it while bouncing a ball?
and so on.

Foot Hoop

Have players link a hoop with one foot and make it go around. See whether they can do this while walking. How about with the other foot? Have them try and toss the hoop to a partner with their foot, to catch on his foot or with his hands.

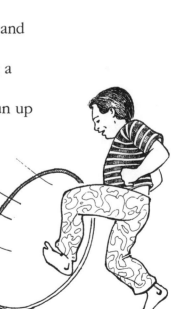

Rolling Runner

Players roll hoops and see whether they can run faster than the hoops to a designated spot, such as the end of the pavement or a line scratched in the earth.

Have them try rolling hoops with both right and left hands.

Try giving the hoop a head start—how long a head start can vary with age and skill level.

Another variation is to give it a start, then run up to it and around it before it falls over.

Hoop-Overs

A player rolls the hoop toward a partner, who leaps over it as it approaches. (See illustration.)

Round Runners

This is a three-player game. Two players stand and roll a large-size hoop to each other. The runner stands to the side, as if they were all playing jump rope and it was the runner's turn to jump in. Instead, the third player tries to run *through* the hoop without touching the side and without disrupting its path to the other person. (See illustration.) Timing is everything!

Another version of this game uses a mat, so that instead of jumping through the moving hoop, the runner can dive through it onto the waiting mat. Adventurous kids particularly enjoy this fling-yourself-into-space version of the game.

Ridiculous Robots

Imagine a circular or linear obstacle course with one or more people on the path acting like robots, raising and lowering a vertically-held hoop while the other players go through the hoops. (See illustration.) Think of a miniature golf layout, where flaps open and close and you have to get the ball through at just the right time. This is a similar idea. The more players you have, the more people can be robots.

The robots can synchronize their movements or get crazy and have each one going at a different speed, each making his own version of what a robot sounds like switching gears.

Not crazy enough yet? Give each robot two hoops.

Round Tag

This is a game for three people. Place three hoops in a circle, far enough apart that players have to **leap** to get from one to the other. One person is "It" and must tag the other two people, but all three must be in a hoop at all times. The trick is for "It" to leap into her neighbor's hoop before her neighbor has a chance to leap out.

Put hoops closer together for younger players.

Rolling Hoops

In this game, two people face each other and roll a hoop back and forth. They can keep increasing the distance between them for added challenge.

Variations:

- Give each person two hoops to roll to his partner; players can choose to set all hoops rolling at once or one set of hoops at a time.

- Put obstacles in the hoop's path, such as pillows, other hoops, shoes, and so on, and roll the hoops from one person to the other over the obstacles. When a hoop hits an obstacle, it makes a satisfying jump, sometimes altering the course of the hoop and forcing the catcher to stay extra alert.

- Roll hoops toward each other with the intention of having the hoops meet and "crash" in the middle.

Playing one variation of these rolling hoop games after another keeps the interest high; introduce the next variation just when (or slightly before) interest in the previous variation begins to fade.

Forward Backward Race

In this race players pair off, with each couple standing back to back inside a hoop, one person facing forward and the other backward. (See illustration.) How do kids like being Pushmi-Pullus?

Have the pairs runs to the goal line and then turn around to run back, so that the one who was running forward is now running backward, and vice versa. This way they can each experience what it feels like to run backward when the person in front is going too fast—a lesson in empathy that might help them take the other person into consideration the next time they are in front.

Step Through

Have the child hold the hoop in front of her horizontally and try different methods of getting inside it. She could step high into the hoop, sling a leg over it, or crawl in from underneath. Any other ways?

Move It Up

This challenge involves stepping into a hoop that's lying on the ground and getting it up and over your head using only a foot.

Memory Maze

In this game the hoops are laid on the ground in any pattern you want. One person makes up the movement of the games: "You jump in the first one, swing your arms in the second, spin around in the third, hop backward on one foot and whistle on the next . . ." making the movements as elaborate or as simple as he wants. (See illustration.)

Variation: Instead of one person making up all the movements, each person adds one. Example: the first person hops in the first hoop and then walks through the others. The second person hops in the first, does a kick in the next, and walks through the others. The third person does a hop in the first hoop, a kick in the second, a frog-like jump to the third, and walks through the others. The game continues until all the hoops have a movement assigned to them and everyone gets at least one chance to do all the movements.

Musical Hoops

In this variation on musical chairs, players move around the room to music while you (or a helper) issue various commands: skip, gallop, hop, run backward, slide, and so on. On the floor around the room are hoops, which the players have to go around or over while moving. When the music stops, players try and land in the hoops. How many people are allowed in each hoop depends upon the number of players and the number of hoops. If you want the group to feel friendlier, set the game up so there are more people per hoop, explaining that the kids will all have to hold on to each other so that everyone inside the hoop is completely contained.

To ensure that there are no losers in this game, it's a good idea for the person who ends up on the outside of the hoops to be the one to choose the movements the players make to the music on the next round. Encourage her to take advantage of her privilege by making up idiosyncratic movements, like, "Jump around with one hand on your backsides and the other on your noses!" Encourage creativity, regardless of how absurd!

Mini-Hurdles

This lightweight, homemade equipment is made out of white PVC pipe and is so versatile that I have been able to work with groups of children ranging from two to twelve years, using mini-hurdles as my only equipment. Jumping, leaping, hopping, and crawling over and under hurdles is wonderful for enhancing a large variety of children's skills, depending on which way the hurdles are placed—upside down, sideways or right side up.

For example, placed upside down with the center bar on the floor, the hurdles can be hopped over. If three hurdles are used, they can become a slalom course.

When the hurdles are placed on their sides, the center bar can be jumped over forward, backward, and sideways. Laid down flat, they can be used as a Hopscotch grid, with children jumping and hopping from one rectangle to the next.

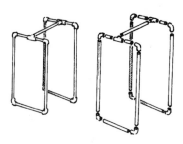

Even the simple act of crawling can take on different dimensions, depending on which way the mini-hurdles are positioned. One position encourages the players to make themselves as narrow as possible, another as flat as possible. One position requires players to slither through, getting even flatter still!

The hurdles can also be used as targets for throwing games. You can disassemble them partway and play ring toss, or set them up one behind another for a 3-D throwing experience. Let your player take them completely apart, and he will be only too glad to come up with a totally new way of putting the pipes back together.

Mini-hurdles are not difficult to make. PVC pipe can be cut with a kitchen knife, and local hardware stores carry all the pipe and joints that are needed. See the illustration for suggestions on how to put them together. The hurdles can be made in a variety of heights so that each fits your child's individual needs.

For a set of mini-hurdles that are eleven inches, fifteen inches, and nineteen inches high, you'll need to cut pieces in the following sizes:

How Many	Size	Purpose
4 pieces	7¾ inches	for 11-inch hurdle
4 pieces	11¾ inches	for 15-inch hurdle
4 pieces	15¾ inches	for 19-inch hurdle
12 pieces	3¾ inches	each hurdle needs 4 pieces

6 pieces	8½ inches	each hurdle needs 2 pieces
3 pieces	16 inches	for the center bar
24 elbow joints	(¾ inches)	8 per hurdle
6 "T" joints	(2¾ inches)	2 per hurdle

The illustration on page 90 shows you how to put it all together.

And this illustration shows you all the many ways these hurdles can be used.

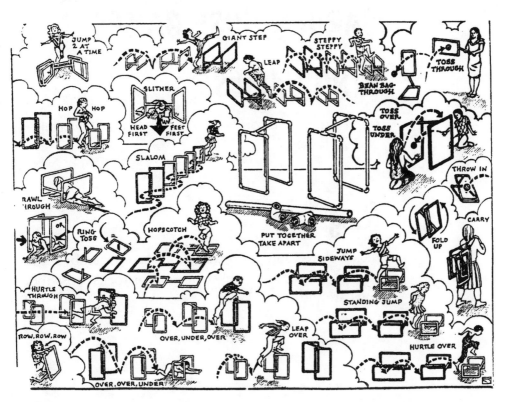

Pipe Fittings

Get a lot of half-inch or three-quarter-inch pipe fittings such as elbow joints, T-joints, and connectors. Then cut up some half-inch or three-quarter-inch PVC pipe and have the player put them together in whatever design strikes his fancy. He may even want to attempt a specific shape or sculpture.

GARDEN HOSE GAMES

RING GAMES

(Find instructions on how to make rings at the beginning of this chapter.)

Ring Toss

Stick a dowel in the ground for a stake or embed a firm newspaper bat in a bucket of sand or rocks. Toss the rings around the stake.

Ring Catch

For small inexperienced hands, a simple game of catch is easier with rings than with balls. Have a few of them ready, so that when your little partner misses one, another is instantly ready without a break in the game or confidence level. After they are all used, you can both gather them up, ring them on your arms like so many bracelets, and start the game of catch and throw again.

Hand Ring

Instead of catching the rings, players can aim their rings at other players' hands and try to ring them.

Bat Catch

Using rings and rolled-up newspapers for a bat (use many layers of newsprint to make it firm) and the garden hose ringers described above, play a game in which one player holds the bat stationary and another player tries to ring it. Or one player can toss the ring and the other player can try to spear it with the bat.

Flying a Plane

Rings are just about the size of a pilot's steering wheel. Teach your player the basic dynamics of steering a plane: that when you pull the wheel toward you, the trees get smaller, and when you push it away, the trees get bigger. Act this out with your movements.

Snake Walk

Lay out some garden hose so it has a series of loops, like a series of cursive "e's." The trick is to walk inside the loops without stepping on the snake!

Twirlers

Use sections of garden hose to make small hoops and then swing them in a circular motion on a finger or wrist or foot.

Shocking Ring

Lay a garden hose in a circle and have players in the center move to whatever directions they are given—hopping, skipping, jumping, etc. The rule is that they are not to touch each other or the garden hose. If they touch either, they get a shock and fall down dead. The dead then become additional electrified obstacles to avoid. Whoever is left standing at the end of the game gets to call out the directions for the next game.

Variation: For an even greater challenge, adjust the hose between movements to make the circle progressively smaller.

Games to play with string, rope, and yarn

STRING AND ROPE are as easy to find as the shoelaces in your jogging shoes. Here are a variety of games in which string or rope is the major or only ingredient. Yarn can be substituted for string if color is preferred.

Broad Jump

Mark a starting spot with a piece of taped string and ask your player to jump as far from that string as possible. Mark the landing spot with another piece of taped string and invite her to try and jump past that string the next time. Continue as long as her legs are willing.

Partner Tug

Tape a length of string on the floor between two people who are about the same size and strength. Ask them to put their hands, palm to palm, against each other, and when you say "go," to start pushing and see who can push who out of the way and step over the line first. Next ask them to link elbows and pull, each trying to pull the other over the line first. Have the same sort of push-pull contest using these body parts:

- back to back

- rear to rear

- rear to rear again, this time bending over and holding each other's hands

- hip to hip

- elbow to elbow

- with an arm under each leg while holding each other's hands (see illustration)

- any of the above while standing on one leg

The benefit of these different positions is that they require strength in different muscles groups, giving each person a chance to shine. If the partners are evenly matched, it's exhilarating for them to have a chance to use their muscle strength to its full extent.

Variety Races

Tape down lengths of string to mark the beginning and end of a race, then try the following:

- Toe races—walking on tiptoes only

- Heel races—walking on heels only

- A rhythmic combination of the first two, such as a toe toe, heel heel, toe toe, heel heel race

- Squatting race

- Walking on the outside edges of your feet race

- Backward running/walking race

- Sideways sliding race

- Gallop race (right or left leg leading)
- Hopping
- Hopping backward

Puzzle

Cut a small square in the middle of a piece of cardboard. Tie a chopstick to each end of a piece of string
and put one chopstick through the hole. Ask your
player to get the string and chopsticks free from the
hole. (See illustration.)

Untangle

Give your child the challenge of untangling something. For the beginner, start with a rope tied in a simple,
loose knot. For the more advanced, use string or yarn.

String Painting

Take a thick pad of paper toweling soaked with paint and
press a piece of string on the pad. Fold half of the towel-

ing over the string and pull it out, making a colored piece of string.

Here are some projects to try with colored string:

- Remove the label from an empty soup or vegetable can, making sure the can is thoroughly rinsed out and clean. Smear the outside of the can with glue. Then make many colors of string and wrap them carefully around the can, one string at a time, until the whole can is covered. This one makes a nice pencil holder.

- Paste colored strings on a piece of cardboard or styrofoam tray to make a picture.

- Lay the strings on a piece of white paper while they are still wet and press another piece of paper on top, making some pretty stationery.

Long-Distance Throws

One string is taped down to mark the foul line, the spot where the player stands; five others are taped down at regular intervals perpendicular to the four line. How far the lines are from the foul line depends on the skill level of your thrower. The player stands on the foul line and throws a beanbag or newspaper ball as far as she can, trying to make it land on or between the strings. If you want to keep score, you can give each line a number. For

example, if the player uses three balls and the first one lands between 3 and 4, it gets 3 points; if the second lands between 4 and 5, it gets four points, and if the third one lands on the number-4 string, it gets 4 points, or 11 points altogether. Each time she plays the game, your player can try to improve her score. Keeping track of points is also a way to help your player see her improvements. "Remember when you started, you were only able to get (number) points, and now you're getting (larger number) points easily!"

Pencil Catch

Tie a pencil to a piece of string and tie the string to a canning jar ring or a plastic lid with the center cut out. The idea is for the child to swing the ring or lid rim and try and try to catch it on the pencil. (See illustration.) Make sure the string is long enough to allow the ring to be flipped over the pencil easily. You can make this progressively harder by using lids of many different sizes; for example, start with a two-pound coffee can lid and progress to baking powder lids or nut can lids.

Beading

Encourage success for the beginner beader by using a thick string or rope as a bead string. The threading end of whatever you use could be stiffened with tape, wax, or glue to make stringing easier. What you use for beads can vary according to your child's ability. Start with a short piece of rope and empty toilet paper rolls or cut up paper towel rolls as beads (see page **141**); canning rings also work well. Progress to things like string and diaper pins, egg carton sections, shower curtain rings, large paper clips, hardware washers, or cut-up straws. Uncooked macaroni wheels and tubes are fun, too—especially the colored ones.

Sideways Jump

Lay a string down and ask your player to jump over it sideways and back a few times. (See illustration.)

Tic-Tac-Toe

Tape string into a giant tic-tac-toe pattern and identify the spaces in between with numbers or letters. If you use letters, ask the player to jump to the letter called, or spell out a word; if you use numbers, have your player memorize a sequence of numbers like 3, 6, 2 and jump to them. You can ask that jumps be done backward, sideways, or forward, depending on the direction needed to go in, or that players hop instead of jumping.

Progressive Jumps #1

Tie one end of a string or rope to something solid and hold the other end. Hold the string down low and ask your player to run and jump over it. Then raise the string a smidgen and ask her to do it again. Each time she jumps, raise the string a little bit more until it is too high to jump over.

Then ask your player to go under it, limbo-style if you want, and keep lowering it until the player has to crawl on her belly, army-combat-style, to get under it without touching it.

> *I have played Progressive Jumps with a wide variety of people, from toddlers to teenagers to developmentally delayed adults. It seems to be a popular game with everyone.*

Progressive Jumps #2

Once players have mastered basic Progressive Jumps, you can move on to more complicated variations. For instance:

- Use two ropes, so that the player has to jump over two ropes in a row.

- Hold two ropes level but apart, so that the player has to jump over a wider area.

- Hold one rope high and the other low so the player has to jump over one rope and go under the other. (See illustration.)

Progressive Jumps #3

If two ropes are even better than one, just think what you could do with three or more. The possibilities are limited

only by the number of humans available to hold the ropes. Here are a few:

- Go over the first, under the second, and over the third; continue this weaving over and under until you run out of ropes.

- Make several double ropes to jump over—some wider, some narrower.

- Stretch them all at slightly different heights so that players have to adjust the height of each jump—good for encouraging motor planning!

- Instead of going over the parallel ropes, the players think of them as aisles, going down one, reversing directions, going down another, and so on.

Simple Jumps

Lay a piece of string or rope down on the floor and ask your player to jump over it. Suggest jumping over other ways—backward, sideways, arms crossed, eyes closed, legs apart, legs together, hands on head, hands behind back, and so on.

Jump the Creek

Lay out two pieces of string or rope close together and parallel, call it a creek, and have players jump over the creek. Move the strings farther apart, change the creek to a brook, and have players jump over the brook; move the strings even farther apart and turn the brook into a river!

If players "get their feet wet," have them pretend to change to dry shoes and socks; if they "fall in the river," they'll need to change their clothes. Kids love these kinds of consequences, and it takes the sting out of failing to make it over the line. You might find on some days that the children purposely "fall in" so they can pretend to change shoes or clothes. That may just mean they're feeling silly and having fun, or it might mean you made the river too wide and need to adjust it back for now.

String Throw

In this game, you and your children throw string in air and catch it. Throw it high. Throw it to a partner. Try juggling with three pieces. After all, when string drops, it doesn't roll away!

Snake

Hold a long piece of string and wiggle it so it writhes enticingly on the floor; ask the child to step on it while you keep moving it around. Have children pair up and try playing this game with each other.

The Path

Make a pathway with two parallel strings or ropes. Start with a wide pathway and make it progressively narrower. Have your young player walk along the path, staying inside the two rows as much as possible. This kind of game is really helpful to a toddler; you know how far apart new walkers keep their legs to ensure that they won't fall. This game gives them a chance to practice walking with a narrower stance.

Older children like to pretend the path is a bridge over turbulent waters filled with sharks and monsters, so they have to work extra hard not to fall in (step outside the lines).

Low Jumps

Tie a rope or a long piece of string between two chairs and have your player run and jump over it; or, if it's low enough to stand in front of, have him jump (or hop) over it forward, backward, and sideways.

Pendulum Game

Why not give your child's eye muscles a workout? Hang an object of interest (a doll, a flower) from a string and swing it from side to side like a pendulum. Ask your player to touch it (or poke it) when you say "now." Encourage her to keep her eyes on the object as it swings.

Pull Toy

Tie a string to a toy and hide the toy under a scarf with the string tantalizingly near your baby. Encourage your little one to pull the string and make the toy reappear.

String Streamers

You and your players each hold a piece of string about twelve to sixteen inches long. Demonstrate a series of movements for them to imitate, such as moving the string like a gymnast's streamer. Move the string in a pattern, such as side to side or up and down. Or you could do a series of rain movements, starting off with a slow up-and-down movement and progressing to a more vigorous up and down one representing a storm. Keep the movement rhythmic and controlled. Ask your players to make up a story or pattern to accompany their actions.

Tickle, Tickle

Blindfold your player or have her close her eyes; then get her to lie on the floor while you tickle her with the end of a piece of string. The idea is for her to guess what part of her body is being ever-so-lightly touched.

Child Wrap-Up

Using yarn or material strips, you wind the children up . . . and then watch as they unwind themselves.

Tug of War

Everyone knows how to play Tug of War: Two teams at opposite ends of a rope try to pull the other team toward them over a marked line. The farther the center line is from where the players start, the more strength will be needed to pull the opposing team over the line.

Variation: In summer, instead of using a marked line, it's a lot of fun to put a small plastic wading pool full of water or a wet plastic sheet in the middle and try to pull each other into the "duck pond" or "creek!"

Tug of Peace

Players get in the usual position for a Tug of War—each half of the group pulling on opposite ends of a rope—except that this time the object is not to see who can pull harder but to see whether they all can go from standing to sitting and back to standing again while keeping the rope taut.

Variation: Make the rope into a square shape with people at each corner pulling it taut. Have them go from sitting to standing while holding the rope in this way.

Horsey

Tie a string around one child's waist, leaving three- to four-foot "reins"; The "rider" holds the ends of the string. When the" rider" says "giddyup" and shakes the reins, the horse goes. When he pulls on the right string, the horse goes right; when he pulls on the left string, the horse goes left. When he tugs both ends, the horse stops. Don't forget to say, "Whoa!"

Tails

In this well-loved game, cut pieces of string long enough so that when one end is tucked into the waist of a child's pants, the the other end will drag along the floor. Tuck a string into the back of each child's pants and call them tails. (Children who have dresses on can have one string tied around their waists and a second tucked into the waist string for a tail.)

The goal is for everyone to run after everyone else trying to step on their tails and pull them out. The challenge is to collect as many tails as you can while still keeping your own. (See illustration.)

This is a great activity when there is excess energy you want to use up!

ROPE ACTIVITIES

Catch of the Day

One person, the "fish," wears gloves and holds on to a rope; the other person, the "fisherperson," hauls in the rope hand over hand, pulling the "fish" in. Instead of a human fish you can also use heavy objects like chairs or books, depending on the strength of the fisherperson.

Beginner's Jump Rope

Teach beginners how to jump rope by dividing the action into two steps: the swing and the jump. Begin by having the child bring the rope overhead and down, stopping it in front of his feet. Then have him jump over the rope. Get him to repeat these steps until he can combine the two actions in a continuous motion.

A thick, rather heavy rope works well for beginners. A lighter rope with knots in the middle will also swing to the floor without tangling.

Knots

Learn how to make simple sailor knots (there are any number of books out there to help you) and teach them to your learner using a thin rope. Bowline knots are especially fun, and I am told that if you can tie a bowline knot with your eyes closed, you can probably get a position as crew on many a cruising yacht.

Tightrope Walk

Lay a length of rope on the floor and invite players to walk along it without falling off, placing one foot in front of the other, heel to toe. Once they get good at that, see whether they can go backward.

Variation: Make the rope curvy, and your players will get more experience in watching what their feet are doing!

Twirling Snake

Hold one end of a rope, stand in the center of a circle, and have the child stand at the perimeter. Then begin turning in complete circles, swinging the rope close to the floor so that the child has to jump over it as it comes by.

Being the one twirling in the center can make a parent dizzy, but children don't seem to have this problem or mind it when they do. Pick a child who is able to keep the rope close to the ground as he twirls so it won't fly up too high and be impossible to jump over quickly.

Gentle Jump

Tie one end of a rope to something stable. Take the other end and gently swing it back and forth low to the floor. Have your player jump over the swinging rope. Hum a song to help her get the rhythm of it: "Jump, jump, jumpy, jump, look at Eliza jumpy-jump."

Alternating Jumps

Make a path by laying down two lengths of rope a short distance apart. Have your player start with his feet close together inside the rope path, then jump, landing with feet apart on the outside of the rope path. Have him do a series of jumps along the path, alternating the open and closed position. (See illustration.)

Snake Catcher

You are the "snake catcher," with a rope about six feet long. Drag the free end of the rope on the ground while your player tries to catch the rope in her hand. (Stop running as soon as your player catches the rope to prevent rope burns.) Now it's your turn to catch the rope while your child is the "snake catcher"!

Kicking Tightrope

Lay down a straight length of rope and place cartons alongside it at short intervals. The trick is to stay on the rope and kick the cartons as you come to them.

Squat Rope Tug

Partners squat down and hold a rope taut between them; then each person pulls on her end of the rope trying to pull the other person off-balance.

Jump Rope Songs

Jumping in time to a song is a wonderful way to encourage rhythmic movement and it's hard to improve on an old favorite:

Teddy Bear, Teddy Bear, turn around

Teddy Bear, Teddy Bear, touch the ground

Teddy Bear, Teddy Bear, shout the news

Teddy Bear, Teddy Bear, show your shoes

Teddy Bear, Teddy Bear, go upstairs

Teddy Bear, Teddy Bear, say your prayers

Teddy Bear, Teddy Bear, turn out the light

Teddy Bear, Teddy Bear, say "Goodnight"

G-O-O-D-N-I-G-H-T!

Spinning Lasso

Tie a large rope into a lasso, and have one of the kids from your group get inside it and cinch the rope *lightly* around his waist. Ask him to spin around while the kids on the outside jump over the moving length of rope. A stuffed sock could be tied to the moving end to weight it down and make it more visible.

CHAPTER SIX

Games to play with cans

Most of these games use aluminum soda cans, which are easy to get. I've even been known to borrow a bunch from a recycling center if I didn't have enough for a game, and then return them later, a little worse for wear!

Can Dumbbells

Have a weight-lifting session using full cans of tomato or other juice as dumbbells. Demonstrate lifting them from shoulder height to straight up over head, and while bending the arms from a straight position to a bent one and back to straight. Then hold them with arms straight out in front and go to an arms-open-wide position, bringing the arms together again.

Do as many "reps" as possible. If large tomato juice cans are too heavy for your child, use smaller cans like beans or soup.

Can Stacking

Give your child empty cans to stack up, one on top of the other, and see how high a tower can be made before it all falls over.

Can Weights

Fill cans that have snug-fitting plastic lids with differing amount of sand or gravel, turn them on their sides so that they will roll, and let the player kick them to a defined target, such as a stationary can. The variations in weight will give your learner experience in using different amounts of strength to kick the cans.

Can Nesting

Find empty cans of different sizes such as cans for peaches, peas, and tomato paste. Clean them well and make sure there are no sharp edges. Paint the cans different colors with lead-free enamel paint, or cover them with contact paper or magazine pictures, if you have the time. Colored tape looks great, and it is fast and easy to apply.

These cans make great stacking and nesting toys for young children and are easy to replace if one gets lost.

Bowling

Set soft drink or other aluminum cans in a pyramid shape and use a ball or bean bag to knock them over. (See illustration.) Remember that the smaller the ball is, the harder the task will be.

Ask your players to count how many were knocked down each time, if counting is a skill that needs reinforcing. After a number of turns, ask how many were knocked down altogether.

English Bowls

Place two or three empty cans in a line facing the bowler, each can one ball's width away from the next. The object is to get the rolling ball as close to the cans as possible *without touching them!* The player to get his ball the closest to a can without touching it wins.

Variation: The first player rolls a ball, and the second player tries to roll her ball so that it nudges the first player's ball into the can and disqualifies it. (See illustration.)

Can Aim

Set up a series of empty cans on top of a table or box and draw a line a few feet away, depending on the skill level of the players. The idea is to knock the cans over using another can as the "ball."

Shell Game

This is a version of the old carnival shell game. For young children, use one large can and one small one and hide a treat (a piece of popcorn, a raisin, a cracker) or an inedible object under one of the cans. Then shuffle the cans

122

around as if you are trying to confuse the child as to which can is covering the treat. Actually all the child needs to notice and learn is whether the treat was under the BIG can or the small one.

For older children, use three identically-sized cans and shuffle them around a lot to see whether they can stay focused and keep track of which can the treat or object is under.

Can Throw

A simple game of "How far can you throw an aluminum can" can be satisfying. See whether your player finds a difference between holding the side of the can and throwing it and holding the end of the can and throwing it. What is the difference in distance between an overhand and an underhand throw?

Wait! Before you go around picking up all those cans, take a look at the next game, "Can Obstacle Course."

Can Obstacle Course

Randomly throw cans all over the floor, or play "**Can Throw**" described above. Then ask your player to run from one end of the room to the other without touching any of the cans. Get him to jump or step over the cans, go around them, or apply a combination of these moves according to your directions.

Kick the Can

This is an old-time rural game, but you can make a country lane by marking a path on the floor using washable felt pens, masking tape, or yardsticks, or outdoors using chalk, sticks, hoses, or rocks. The path can be short, straight, and wide for beginners, or long, curvy, and narrow for those who need more of a challenge. The idea is to start at one end and kick the can to the other end, keeping control over the can so that it stays within the lines.

For added skill, place obstacles in the road for the can to go around.

Can Flatteners

If cans are flattened before being recycled in your community, why not make a game out of it? Remove the ends of vegetable and soup cans and lay them out on their sides for players to jump on.

For aluminum soda cans, line cans up in a path and have the players stomp on their ends as they walk along.

Home Base

Put one can down as Home Base and set up three others at different distances and directions from the first. It's helpful to use different brands of soft drinks.

The player stands by the Home can and notes exactly where the other cans are placed. Now ask her to walk, with eyes closed, directly to the root beer can, for example, pick it up, and go back home. Do this until all the cans are picked up.

Variation: With her eyes still closed, ask the player to go from one can to the others named without returning to Home first.

Can Course

Set up a series of cans and have players take turns kicking another can around them in the pattern you designate. For example, tell them to go around each can once or twice or weave in and out of a row of cans.

Stilts

Stilts are easy to make. Take two large empty cans, such as tomato juice cans or two-pound coffee cans, and poke two (parallel) holes in the bottom of each one close to the edge. Thread a long rope through the holes for the stilt walker to hold onto, knotting it at each end so it can't slip back through the holes. Now the player can walk on the cans holding onto the ropes like reins.

(Don't do this barefoot or in socks. It's easier on the feet to wear shoes when walking on can tops!)

Stepping Stone Cans

Using a variety of size cans, especially the larger ones, make a path so players can walk from one can to another.

If some of the cans squash as they are walked on, consider it a challenge to their balance, but stay nearby to lend a supporting arm.

Erratic Kick

Place cans randomly around the room. At the signal the player has to run around the room kicking over each can.

The trick is to do it as quickly as possible, meaning the player must plan her route as effectively as possible.

Variation: If you use a stack of cans at each spot instead of just one, they'll make a much more rewarding sound when kicked. And all those rolling cans will serve as extra obstacles to be dealt with.

Maracas

Fill juice cans that have plastic snap-on lids with different materials so they make different sounds. These are your maracas. Have your learners distinguish between playing loudly and softly, slowly and rapidly.

The five remaining games in this chapter are designed to be played one after another. When I am trying to lead a tightly organized class, I make sure each game leads right into the next, so kids will not get distracted between activities and start wrestling or fooling around. The sequence that follows works particularly well.

Can Tower Relay

Cans are placed on one end of the room, children at the other. At the signal, each child must run to the other side, get a bunch of cans, run back, build a tower, run and get more, and so on, with the goal being to build as high a tower as they can as fast as they can. If the activity is done twice, consider using a timer for the fun of seeing whether the children can build their towers faster the second time.

Can Throw

After the "Can Tower Relay" towers fall over, have children throw cans as far as they can. This helps vent any frustrations that might have arisen if towers kept falling over.

Obstacle Run

With the cans from "Can Throw" scattered all over the floor, have your children run from one end of the room to the other without running into or in any way touching any of the cans.

Can Squash

Children again run back and forth across the room, except that this time they try and land *on* the cans!

Can Pickup

Children run from one end of the room to the other, gathering up cans as they go and seeing how many they can pick up and put into a box at the other end of the room.

Okay, you and I know this is our way of getting the room cleaned up, and the kids must know it too—but for some weird and wonderful reason they go for it every time. Just like that the room that had been covered with cans (or lids or milk cartons) is suddenly clean! Try it.

Games to play with paper

These games call for all sorts of paper products, including magazines, used photocopy paper, grocery bags, and scrap paper. Used paper products are such a regular part of everyday life, it's satisfying to get some free play out of them instead of just throwing them away!

Action Cards

Write all the numbers from five to twenty on separate index cards or small slips of paper. On another set of cards, write the names of a variety of actions. Examples: skip, hop, jump, twirl, bounce, rotate, jump, run backward, giant steps, thrust, slash, swish, flick, press, push, slip, dab, jerk, drag, perch, slide, kick backward, bunny hop.

Players take turns picking a card from each pile. The players must perform the action on the movement card the number of times stated on the number card.

I start with the number five because it's not that much fun to do a movement just a few times. But choose the numbers and actions according to the attention span and skill level of your group.

Variation: You can also use description on the movement cards such as "move like an alligator" (or a crab or a lame dog or a spider or a frog or a duck or an elephant or a snowball or an inchworm or even an elevator!).

Paper Faces

Have each child draw a pair of matching faces on two sheets of used paper. The format should be a simplified, eyes-eyebrows-nose-and-mouth kind of design, and the expressions on the faces should differ. One child might draw a pair of happy faces, another a pair of angry faces, others frustrated, sad, proud, or sleepy faces.

These faces can be used in three different ways.

Active. This is a jumping game. The papers are laid on the floor face side up. Someone calls out an emotion, and the player has to jump to the face that has the expression named, then jump from there to the matching face, regardless of how far away that face is from its match.

Dramatic. Children act out movements that depict the emotion on the face. Walk briskly with anger or shuffle along sadly; reach out with longing or stomp with frustration.

Quiet. This is the memory game sometimes called "Concentration." The papers are laid face down on the table, and two are turned over on each turn. If two matching ones are turned over, that pair is removed from the set. If they don't match, the papers are turned over again and the next person has a turn.

Movement Categories

Cut out magazine pictures that depict action of any sort—eating, running, reading, watching television, playing, etc.

Show the pictures to the players and ask them what the person in the picture is doing. They might want to imitate the action or even make up a story about what they see.

As a variation, show each picture to just one player and have her imitate the action while the others try to guess what she's doing. The first one to guess gets the next turn.

Paper Games

Use a variety of paper: tissue, grocery bag, butcher paper, wrapping paper, shelf paper, shirt cardboard, paper plates, waxed paper, cellophane, foil, newspaper, doilies, and placemats.

Let your children have fun working with the paper in a variety of ways: cutting, tearing, crinkling, waving, tossing, crumpling, coloring, folding, flapping, or stuffing it in a sock or milk carton.

Possible games:

- How fast can you tear up a paper bag into small shreds?

- How many shapes can you tear out of wax paper?

- How far can you throw a ball made out of foil? out of newspaper? out of tissue paper? out of cellophane?

- Can you throw an uncrumpled piece of paper into the air and catch it as it comes floating down?

- Can you make a paper plate into a flying saucer?

- Have the children experiment with fringes. Using scissors, snip a one-inch fringe around the edge of a paper or tear a fringe with fingers. Mark heavy lines where your player should cut or tear, if needed.

Try making paper chains out of different kinds of paper. Have the children cut the various papers into strips. Form the first strip into a circle and glue it; then thread the next strip through the first and glue it. You can make your chains as long as you like. When you're finished, hang them up for decorations!

Catalog Browsing

Give children old catalogs for page-turning experience as well as for tearing. For more elaborate play, provide sheets of scrap paper, safety scissors, and glue and allow children to create their own collages.

Grocery Bag Mask

Make a mask out of a bag by tearing bits and pieces out of it. (See illustration.)

Blind Drawing Game

Give your players pencils and paper and ask them to draw something in the room without looking down at their paper while they are drawing. Results are especially amusing if the children happen to be drawing portraits of each other.

Design Drawing

Put on some music. Give each player a pencil or a pen and ask the children to draw designs on the paper to match the mood of the music. Point out that they should not try to draw something recognizable, but simply move the pencil or crayon around any which way.

Then, using crayons, colored chalk, pastels, or felt markers, have them color in the spaces their lines made. Encourage them to stay within the lines, if possible.

Variation: Instead of using music, you could just ask them to scribble on the page or make free-form doodles, then color in the spaces.

Shape Figures

Ask your players to draw a square on a clean sheet of paper. Then ask them to turn their squares into things. For example, a square could be turned into a train, a jack-in-the-box, a car, or a robot head.

Do the same thing with other shapes. Or use several shapes at once. What can be drawn out of a square, triangle, and circle?

Shelf Paper

Buy a roll of plain shelf paper. Unroll it in front of a group of children armed with crayons and felt markers, and let them at it! The only rule for this activity is for children to keep their artistic efforts confined to the paper and not to draw on top of anyone else's work.

The final results can be displayed on the wall and then rolled back up and used as gift-wrapping paper.

Puzzle Matches

Paste magazine pictures on pieces of cardboard or heavy paper, taking care to cover the entire surface of the cardboard with a thin coating of glue or paste. Then cut the pictures up into odd shapes. How many pieces and how odd the cuts depends on the age of the child. Start with a picture cut in half for the toddler.

Now give her the cut-up pieces from several pictures and ask her to find the matching pieces and put the puzzles together.

Variation: Instead of cutting the pictures into smaller pieces, cut them in half, show one half to the player, and have her guess what the other half looks like; or give her the mixed-up halves and see whether she can match them. Finally, experiment with putting the top half of one picture with the bottom half of another and see what you come up with!

Scissor Work

Most children enjoy experimenting with using scissors. Draw a pair of heavy lines on a piece of paper (the lines should not cross) and have your learner try and cut between the lines. Another idea is for children to cut out circles from the center of a sheet of paper or a paper plate. For the beginner, you hold the paper and turn it as the child cuts. Once that is mastered, ask your beginner to cut out wavy lines, spirals, and fringes. Experiment with cutting other things too, like lettuce leaves, potato peels, and dried leaves.

Drawing

Drawing is always fun, but it's even more fun to have a variety of things to draw on. Tape a large piece of butcher or computer paper or an open bag on the floor, or get a pile of used photocopy paper from any office. What else can be drawn on?

Paper Weaving

Take a paper bag and cut slits in the sides, leaving the bag intact at the top and bottom. (See illustration.) Then cut strips of colored paper out of construction paper or wrapping paper or even magazine pictures.

Weave these strips in and out of the slits in the paper bag to get a kind of Easter basket effect.

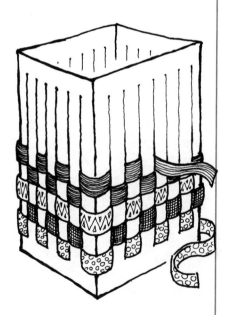

Paper Puppets

Draw figures with your children on a piece of heavy paper, cut them out, and mount them on wooden popsicle sticks or tongue depressors. Use yarn for hair and scrap material for clothes. Put on a show!

Tear-a-Shape

Use a variety of paper—tissue paper, butcher paper, wrapping paper, shelf paper, shirt cardboard, paper plates, wax paper, tinfoil, construction paper, and bond paper. Depending on the finger strength of your players, choose some of these papers and ask the children to tear out shapes. Beginners will want to tear out squares and other easy shapes, while more advanced players might want to try for a person or animal.

If you suggest a theme such as "Animals," "Vehicles," or "Fun Things for Summer" you could have them paste the results onto a large collage at the end.

Toilet Roll Beads

I admit the name is not all that inviting, but cutting up toilet paper rolls into small sections make great beads for the beginning beader. The bead string with beads of this size can even be a rope, so that clumsy or inexperienced fingers can do quite well.

If you want to make the beads more appealing, cover the rolls with contact paper before cutting them up.

You can also cut up paper towel rolls.

Paper Cup Toss

This is just like "Yogurt Toss #1" on page 66, except that it uses paper cups. A nice way to get some use out of those used picnic cups!

Tube Swords

The tubes from paper towel rolls make decent swords for fencing. Use this with players who have fairly good control, so that they will more likely hit each other's sword rather than each other.

Tube Catch

Tie a canning jar ring to one end of a piece of string; fasten the other end of the string to a paper towel tube. The object is to flip the canning ring up and onto the tube.

Tube Walk

Give each player three paper towel tubes. Have them walk along holding two of the tubes and balancing the third one on the other two.

Flying Plates

Paper plates, especially the more durable ones, make fine flying saucers. Sail the saucers back and forth with your kids, or set up a line of milk or yogurt cartons to be knocked down by the harder paper plates. The lighter-weight plates are good for throwing and catching because they are more unpredictable, meaning the catcher has to run around trying to be in the right place at the right time.

Used paper plates can be found after parties. (Look for ones that are still relatively clean.) A great way to get one more use out of the plates before they are returned to the earth.

Footprint Game

Give each child a piece of paper and ask him to stand on it while you or he outlines his feet. Make many footprints,

outlining sometimes both feet, sometimes only one. The
children can color the feet shapes in, if they want.

Then lay the footprints out in a long line.
If the first paper has two feet on it, the player jumps
onto the paper; if the next one has only foot, the
player hops onto that piece. If the footprints are close
together, it indicates baby jumps or hops; if they are
far apart, giant jumps or hops will be needed.

Older kids could distinguish between a left
foot and a right foot.

Variation: Make outlines of hands too, sometimes
one hand, sometimes both. Include them in the line so
that children may have to hop on one paper and then
while balancing on one foot, reach down and put two
hands on the paper in front of them and them jump over
that paper to the two footprints on the next paper.

Children can take turns laying out the papers so
that they can directly affect the movements required.

Used photocopy paper is perfect for this game.

If you want to use these feet patterns for more
than one game, cover them with clear contact paper or
laminate them with adhesive plastic, and they will last
awhile.

Instead of using separate sheets of paper, a series
of foot and hand prints can be made on long roll
of butcher or shelf paper. Make more than one variation.

Photocopy Paper Jumps

Used photocopy papers are taped down in a random pattern so that the length of the jumps from paper to paper will be varied: some long, some short, and some impossible (but ask them to try for it anyway; the impossible is always a good stretch!).

Include other movements as well, such as hopping, backward jumping, jumping and twirling, leaping, and so on.

Paper Target

Draw a target on a piece of paper. A giant black dot will do. Then tape that paper to the wall a couple of feet from the floor, and ask your player to kick something and aim for the target. That something could be a newspaper ball (see chapter 2), a milk carton block (see chapter 3), or even a ball.

Blind Walk

You remember this game. One person closes her eyes and is led by a friend around the room or yard on a long, trusting walk. Trusting, that is, that the leader won't lead the "blind" person into a table! Because it is hard to keep ones' eyes closed and not cheat, I suggest placing a paper grocery bag over the "blind" player's head. You can draw a face on the bag to make it more appealing.

It's interesting for the leader to stop every so often and ask the "blind" person whether she knows where she is. Near the oak tree? By the book shelf?

Hug a Tree Walk

If you have trees and some yard, here's a variation on "Blind Walk." The leader takes the "blind" player on a circuitous route ending at a tree, then asks her to feel or hug that tree before being returned to the starting point by an equally circuitous journey.

Then the bag is removed, and the formerly "blind" player is asked to go find that tree. The player might need to hug a number of trees to find the one that feels familiar. The trees won't mind a bit!

Blind Pick-Up

Place a piece of balled-up paper in the middle of the room and have the player note the location before placing a bag over his head. Then ask your child to walk directly toward the paper and pick it up. It's harder than it sounds, so be sure to take your turn at this game and find out what your kids are up against!

Keep changing the location of the ball so that sometimes it's directly in front of the player and sometimes on a diagonal path, sometimes close and sometimes far away.

Bagheads #1

This game uses as many large paper grocery bags as there are players, minus one. Start by putting a bag over somebody's head. "Baghead" then tries to tag any of the other children, who in turn try to stay out of reach but inside the boundary lines. When another player is tagged, that person puts on a bag and becomes a "baghead." Now there are two bagheads to avoid.

The game continues until only one person is left bagless. That person becomes the first baghead for the next game.

If the bagheads are having a hard time finding people because the room is so large, you can try one of two things: Reduce the size of the boundaries, or ask the others to keep calling out to the bagheads to give them sound clues to follow.

I often find that instead of trying not to be tagged, the other players will seek it out. It seems some people just like to have a bag over their head. Go figure.

Bagheads #2

In this version of Bagheads, only the person who is "It" has a bag on her head. The other players are free to run around until the person who is "It" says, "Freeze!" At this point, every player stands still while "It" wanders around trying to find someone. When she does, she has to guess who it is by feeling that person. If she guesses correctly, that person becomes the new "It" and the games continues. If she guesses incorrectly, all the other players go back to running around until "It" calls out "Freeze!" and tries again.

Backward Walking

Walking or running backward across a cleared floor is always a little scary. Doing it with eyes closed or a grocery bag over your head adds to the thrill!

Stand at the ending spot and call out the children's names as they come backwards into your arms. It's always nice to get a little hug after doing some dangerous trick!

Toilet Paper Wrap

Although for obvious reasons this game requires new materials, it's worth including, as it's a fairly inexpensive game for the amount of fun it produces.

Players wrap each other up in toilet paper from neck to ankles so that their arms are at their side and their feet together. When players are fully mummified, hold a jumping race, or have them perform maneuvers such as jumping around a series of obstacles. Or just let them jump around by themselves until they break free from their paper cocoons.

Grocery Bag Kick

Players start at a designated spot with one foot in a grocery bag. They then kick the leg that is in the bag, causing the bag to fly off their leg and land on the floor. If the bag lands on its side, they put one leg in again and kick it further along. The goal can be another designated spot about twenty or thirty feet away.

If, however, the bag lands on its bottom, the player is allowed to get in the bag and jump five jumps toward the goal. After the five jumps, they have to begin the one-leg-kick routine again.

148

Grocery Bag Jump

Players stand in grocery bags and jump from one spot to another. This game can be set up as a race or timed for people's personal best.

Other grocery bags can be laid on the "track" as obstacles to jump over.

Grocery Bag Throw

One of the by products of "Grocery Bag Jump" is torn bags. These can be balled up and thrown into the bags that didn't get torn. It's a good way to clean up the area after the jumping game, as well as a chance for some throwing fun.

Grocery Bag Fight

This is another use for torn grocery bags. Partners flail at each other's bag with no particular point— apart from the joy of flailing!

I don't approve of fighting, but some little boys I know seem to cherish the sport and will take any opportunity to test themselves against another male. In this game, the rule is that bags can only hit other bags, not anyone's flesh.

The bags are torn beyond use fairly quickly, so this game serves as a fast way to release energy before the next game begins.

Grocery Bag Slide

Place unopened grocery bags on the floor and see how many ways your children can move on their bags. Skating? Sitting? Sliding? Balancing? Moving in different shapes?

Watch what ideas the players come up with and then suggest they all imitate another's idea.

Grocery Bag Obstacles

Arrange unopened bags on the floor, evenly spaced in no certain pattern. Using taped music or a drum beat, have players move around these obstacles by running, tiptoeing, sliding sideways, walking, crawling, jumping, moving on backs or stomachs, hopping, skating, twirling, walking backwards and so on.

Ask your player(s) whether they can move between and around the bags without touching even a tiny corner of a them.

Paper Pickup

In this game, the player stands in front of a balled-up piece of paper, leans forward, and picks up the paper with her teeth. If possible, have her keep her hands behind her back. If not, her hands can be used to provide support.

Variation: Form teams of two. One person picks up the paper with his teeth and passes it to his partner's teeth. That person then runs to a designated container and drops the ball into it.

Grocery Bag Challenge

- How many ways can you get into a bag without using your hands?

- How many parts of the body can you wear a bag on? How many ways can you move when the bag is there?

Bag I.D.

In this game one player wears a grocery bag over her head, while the others take turns coming up and standing in front of her. The bagged person's task is to try and guess who is standing there by the sense of touch—judging size, shape, length of hair, and so forth. The person standing in front should keep quiet to ensure that the clues are all tactile ones. If the player is having a hard time identifying her subject, have that person say something and add voice recognition to the game. He could even disguise his voice to add to the challenge. Once the person is identified, he becomes the next to be bagged.

Variation: I like to sing a song while the identifying is going on to keep all the players involved. The song I sing is to the tune of the old Campbell's soup commercial that went: "um, um, good, um, um, good,/ that's what Campbell's soup is, um, um, good." Except the words I use are, "Who is this? Who is this? /Can you tell us who this is?". If you're not old enough to remember the Campbell's soup tune, make up one of your own.

Blind Ball

Have the children sit in a circle and ask them to look around and try to memorize who is sitting where. Then have each person place a paper bag over his head for a blind game of ball.

In this game, whoever has the ball first calls out the name of the person the ball is being rolled to, then attempts to roll the ball in that person's direction. The player who gets the balls calls out his name, so everyone will know who it went to, and then calls out the name of another person and rolls the ball.

Animal Partners

This is another two-part game. In the first part the children make masks by drawing pictures of animal faces on grocery bags.

In the second part, half the children put on their masks and the rest make the sounds of the animals portrayed. Each of the masked kids has to find her partner.

This game requires some organization, as you quietly assign each person to a partner. Sean has a dog mask, so you tell Jennifer that she is to bark until Sean finds her; Eliza is wearing an elephant mask, so Josh has to make elephant sounds until he is found.

Whether you want the masks to have eye holes in them, or whether you want the children to rely totally on sound, will depend on the skill level of your group.

Remind the children, when they are making their masks, to choose animals that make sounds, unless you want the game to use mainly movement for identification. A scorpion, a crab, a deer, an elephant, and an ape are all animals that could be found by their characteristic movements.

Crepe Paper Streamers

Finally, a use for the leftover crepe paper from a birthday party!

- Issue two five or six-inch lengths of crepe paper per player. Play music and have the players move around the room anyway they want, incorporating the streamers into their movement.

- Pair or group the players and have them make up a dance using the streamers.

- Let them decorate and wrap their bodies with streamers and used crepe paper. Suggest they move around the room, inspired by how these decorations make them feel. (See illustration.)

- Have each person make a design on the floor with his streamers, and then move around the design in different ways: dancing, hopping, jumping, and so on. (See illustration.)

- Lay streamers on the floor in a design and have players copy the designs with their bodies on the floor next to them. (See illustration.)

- Attach the streamers to sticks and move them in a stylized fashion: figure eights, arm rotations in the same or opposite direction, side to side, or up and down.

- Have them make up short routines to perform for each other.

Make sure each child has a large space to work in.

Musical Paintings

Play a variety of music—calypso, reggae, classical, jazz, rock, and so on—and have your learners paint what they hear. For example, they might paint fast, short strokes when the music is quick, and long, languid strokes when the music is flowing.

Cooperative "Pin the Tail"

First the children draw and color an animal on a large sheet of paper. Part of the group colors the picture while the other part makes a paper tail.

The game itself is the same as ordinary "Pin the Tail," except that the group calls out directions to help the blindfolded person put the tail in the right place. They say things like, "To the right," "Go up," and so on.

Variation: Instead of a cutout of an animal the players could outline the body of one of the players, creating facial features and clothes to pin on instead of a tail.

A nice thing about this version is that everyone get to add something different.

Don't be surprised when the directions that are given purposely call for an arm to be pinned on the head and the eyes on the knee cap! Children love the ridiculous.

Cooperative Puzzle

Take a piece of paper and tear or cut it into as many pieces as you have players. The players then work together to put their pieces back into the original paper shape.

Games to play with cardboard boxes

Any parent who's had the experience of watching a child forego the expensive Christmas toy in favor of the huge box it was shipped in knows what this chapter's all about. Cardboard boxes are cheap, fun, and easy to manipulate. All you have to add is imagination.

Good sources for boxes: grocery, liquor, and shoe stores, where they are usually piled high and free for the asking. Check with department stores, too, for boxes used to ship washing machines and other large appliances.

The Big Train Ride

IMPORTANT: Close adult supervision required: watch for stairs and other hazards!

Clear a large area so that it is free of obstacles. A big cardboard box is the train. The Rider, sitting in the box, holds on to a rope, while the Pulled holds on to the other end of the rope and pulls the train.

For added challenge, try this variation. Place a large paper grocery bag over the Puller's head and instruct the Rider to give the Puller directions. Can the team make it from the couch to the toy box at the other end of the room? How long does it take? Be careful to monitor for movement toward stairs, doors, and other potential trouble spots as the game proceeds.

Remind the Rider that the instructions have to be good ones: The players change places next time around!

Box Walk

In this game each player gets a cardboard box to stand in. Players then have to jump and wiggle to get their boxes from one end of the room to the other without getting out of them.

Jump Off

Sturdy reinforced cardboard boxes make good platforms for beginning jumpers to jump from. Make a path of them and have the jumper climb on the first one and jump off, then climb to the second one and jump off, continuing until the end.

Use a timer or a stopwatch if your little one would like to see whether she can do it more quickly on the next try.

Square Moves

How many ways can you make a square move? Cut cardboard squares from the sides of boxes and ask your children how many different ways they can move the squares across the room. (See illustration on next page.)

- "Sit on it with your legs straight in front and then bend your legs toward you as you pull yourself forward. You're rowing a boat!"

- "Sit on it backward and push off with your legs to propel yourself forward. You're in reverse!"

- "Stand behind it, bend down, and put both hands on it. Run forward: You're a race car!"

- "Put one leg on it and push yourself along with the other. You're riding a scooter!"

- "Kneel on it and pull yourself along with your hands. You're a turtle!"

- "Put one foot on it and pivot around with the other foot. You're a spinning top!"

- "Bend over and put your hands on the paper; push your hands forward and then walk your feet forward. Repeat, repeat, repeat. You're an inch worm!"

What other ways are there to move? Let the players experiment and then have them imitate each other's movements. Can they give their movement a name?

You can varnish the squares or cover them with contact paper if you want to make them to last or look pretty.

Push and Flop

A child pushes a cardboard box quickly across a smooth floor, and once he has got it going, flops his body on top of it for the rest of the ride. This is not the kind of activity adults would think of but when Tyler came up with it in a class of children, they all were eager to try it.

Back Push

In this one the child lies in a box on her back with her legs hanging over the side. Then she uses her feet to push the box backward across the room. (See illustration.)

Box Toss

Picking up a cardboard box and hurling (or heaving) it forward like a shot put develops arm strength and encourages children to identify with Superman, especially if the hurling is done with one arm.

Box Flip: Throwing a box into the air in such a way as to cause it to twirl is another body strengthener.

Box Bang: Toss one box up in the air and, while it is up there, hit it with another box. This game doesn't take much in the way of aim, but it does require strength and timing. It also makes a satisfyingly loud "thump!" when the two boxes collide.

Box Roll

One day a young boy named Eric brought a long narrow box to class. Maybe an upright vacuum cleaner came in it, I don't know. Anyway, Eric's idea was to get inside and roll around, which was a great sight—a box rolling along as if on its own volition. His brother Kelvin wanted a turn, but since they had been fighting earlier, Eric was not giving up his box; besides he was having a great time. We could hear him giggling inside. Kelvin got to join in the fun anyway, though. As the giggling, rolling box came toward him, he jumped over it to get out of the way, and then, realizing what fun that was, continued running back and forth, jumping over the rolling box as it made its way across the gym floor. If the children take turns rolling and jumping, they'll have twice as much fun.

Marble Arches

Cut off the four top flaps of a cardboard box and place it upside down on the floor. Use a knife (a steak knife works well) to cut out some arches or small doors in the sides of the box. Make some openings nice and wide and others narrower. Sit with your player a short distance away and flick or shoot marbles or ping-pong balls into the openings. (See illustration.)

For an added dimension, give each opening a numerical value and then add up the score afterward. Everyone who plays is on the same team, so you all add up your points together for one big score.

Cardboard Purse

Cut out the sides of a cardboard box to make four rectangles. Punch holes around three sides of each piece. If a hole puncher can't do the job, use a pencil (your job!). Then have your worker lace two of them together using yarn or string. Wrap tape around the end of the string to make it stiff, like a needle. In the end you have more of a portfolio than a purse, but it can be used to hold your learner's favorite pictures.

Cardboard Picture

This is like the "Cardboard Purse" activity, except that the holes are placed in the center of the cardboard side and the worker threads the yarn in and out to make a design or a picture. (See illustration.) If you cut off the sides of the box for this activity rather than leaving the box intact, it's easier for little hands.

Cardboard Paintings

The sides of cardboard boxes make a nice sturdy "paper" to use poster paint on, since it doesn't tear. You could even mark a one-inch space along the edge to create an instant frame.

Cardboard Easel

Cut off the corner of a box to make a handy easel. (See illustration.)

Toss in the Box

Lay out boxes of different sizes on the floor and mark a place for the throwers to stand. Have them see how many balls, bean bags, pebbles, etc., they can throw into the boxes. If you use a scoring system, award them more points for the smaller boxes.

Box Bottom Frisbees

I am always on the lookout for different things to throw, both for the sake of variety and to decrease dependence on balls. Box bottoms work well. These nice, flat rectangles are safe to throw and easy to aim. Try setting up targets, like stuffed animals or empty plastic bottles, and inviting players to knock them off a table or other surface.

Kick Box

Cut both ends off of a box and lay it on its side. Ask the children to kick a ball through the box.

Set up several boxes of differing sizes for a game of miniature golf, except, of course, that children use their feet instead of golf clubs. Tennis balls, golf balls, and beach balls all work well for this game. The bigger the box, the lower the par for that course.

Nesting Boxes

It's surprisingly easy to get shoe and boot boxes from shoe stores, and they make good nesting boxes. Children's shoe boxes fit into adult size shoe boxes, which fit into boot boxes. This activity teaches young ones about sizes: Little things fit inside big things. Older kids can hide a present in the smallest box, put that box inside the other two boxes, wrap it up, and give it to someone for a surprise present. If they decorate all three boxes first, so much the better!

Box Tunnel

By opening up both ends of a series of large boxes, you can make a neat tunnel to crawl through.

Box Drag

There are many ways to make a box move, some of which have already been noted. In this activity, children stand with one foot in a box and the other on the floor, and walk and drag the box along as quickly as they can, either in a straight line or following a path. Can they think of other ways to make the box move?

Hang Ten

In this game, one child is in the box while another person pushes or pulls it. The child in the box can be sitting or, if she wants to challenge her sense of balance, standing! It's great practice for would-be surfers!

Box Balance

Have the child place the flat bottom of a large box on his head and walk, trying to keep the box from tumbling off.

Box Dance

The child stands in a box, you put on some music, and your dancer jiggles and bounces and two-steps around, making the box jiggle and move around, too.

Box Pile

In this closely supervised game, the player piles some boxes on top of each other, climbs to the top of them, and balances: King or Queen of the Mountain!

Box Walk

Use those sturdy, coated cardboard boxes that produce comes in. Turn them upside down and let your player walk from one to another. You can put the boxes close together at first, then increase the distance between them.

Mashed Box

Lay three shoe boxes on the floor to form an obstacle course. The first two boxes are right side up; the third is upside down. The object is to jump into the first box and then jump out of it, run around the second box twice and then jump *on* the third box, mashing it. (Kids tend to like that part the best!). The mashed box then becomes the second box, the one that is run around, while the second box takes the third spot. Get it? Continue until all available boxes are demolished.

Flying Jumps

A delicate little four-year-old girl named Mona came up with this game, which I thought exceedingly brave of her. She'd take a running start toward an empty cardboard box and then jump into it, maintaining an upright balance.

Once in the box she'd start jumping around, causing the box to move forward. The other children were only too glad to imitate her idea!

Kid in a Box

See how tightly players can curl up their bodies to fit inside boxes of different sizes. Can they make themselves so small that the box could be turned upside down or on its side with them in it? Could another player find which box they were in among a lot of overturned boxes? (See illustration.)

What Else

This is an imagination game in which you and your child try to think of all the things your box could be. A spaceship? A donkey cart? A boat? A carnival ride? Mime the movements or "play pretend" for each idea that appeals to you.

Paid TV

A young boy named Alden does this game at home: Using a large box like the kind refrigerators or washing machines come in, he cuts a hole for a TV screen, goes inside, and performs for his family. No fool he, he also cuts a slot in the box where they insert money to make the show begin! You don't have to suggest this to your child, of course, if it's not your taste. He probably won't think it up on his own. Or, if you like, you could make pretend coins out of cardboard and let him cash them in for extra dessert!

Wheels

Draw wheels on the sides of a box or cut them out of another cardboard box and attach them. Now you have a stagecoach, a racing car, a donkey cart, a mini-van—whatever your player wants—and a whole scenario can be made up to go along with it.

Turtle

A little girl named Maddie figured out that if you put a box over your crawling body, you could turn into a moving turtle. Since Maddy was the youngest in a class whose ages ranged from four to ten years, she found that going around as a turtle was a fun way to be part of the group and not have to interact on a day she was feeling less social than usual.

In a whole group of small ones you could turn everyone into turtles. You could even make peep holes in the front of their boxes so that you don't end up with a turtle version of "bumper car."

Everybody In!

If you have one of those large boxes refrigerators come in, let a group of kids see how many of them they can fit into the box.

You might think this activity would be too uncomfortable to bother with, but children enjoy it a lot. (Wasn't there some fad where college students tried to see how many could fit into a phone booth?) It might be best if children removed their shoes for this one, so that no one gets kicked too hard.

Box Car Derby

If you have a smooth floor and empty cardboard boxes, this game is a natural. Each kid grabs a box and runs madly around the room, pushing her box ahead of her. When I let a group of kids weave in and out and around each other on their own, without giving them any directions, they race around, pushing their boxes, making sounds, and having a grand old time. To the adults on the sidelines, it all looks rather pointless; but, then I guess needing things to have a point is a sign of age anyway.

Jukebox

Using a large, refrigerator-sized box, cut a flap in one side that can be opened from inside of the box. Make a slit beside the flap. One child gets inside the box; another slips a piece of paper with the name of the song on it through the slot. The child inside has to lift the flap and sing the requested song.

I saw a street musician do this one at Fisherman's Wharf in San Francisco. He was a big hit.

Jukebox Quiz

This is like "Jukebox" except that the person in the box keeps changing. Have children close their eyes while you silently choose someone to get inside the box. Whoever it is does not lift the flap, but just sings a song or says some words; the other students then have to guess who is inside of the box.

CHAPTER NINE

Games to play with unmatched socks

Finding a ball when you need one can be a challenge in itself. Balls have a tendency to vanish when no one is looking, not unlike the sock that disappears somewhere between the washing and drying. Now there's one solution to both of these problems—sockballs! Take two or three unmatched socks, depending on their thickness, and roll them up to make a sockball. (See illustration.) Put beans in the toes and tie off the top for an instant bean bag, or use sand to make weights. Gravel—the kind used in fish tanks—also makes good filler, with the advantage that gravel bean bags can be thrown in the washing machine. (Beans tend to sprout when they're washed!)

A number of newspaper ball games listed in chapter 1 also works well with sock balls. For example, try "A Step at a Time" on page 20, "Upside-Down Roll" on page 21, "Ball Toss" on page 23, "Partner Toss" on page 24, "Baseball," "Golf," and "Croquet" on pages 25 and 26, "Stair Toss" on page 28, "Kangaroo Ball" on page 29, and "Running the Gauntlet" on page 43.

Hit The Buns and Run

Lay sockballs around on the floor. (Don't use beanbags stuffed with beans or sand.) When someone shouts, "Go for the buns," everyone grabs a sockball and aims it at the nearest *gluteus maximus*. Players can give themselves a score for each hit, but they will probably be too busy running toward the next sockball while trying to protect their own posteriors.

You'll know when the game is over—players will be lying exhausted on the floor or ground, panting but happy.

This is an especially good game to play when there are a wide range of ages in the group because there is so much action one can't tell who is doing what or how accurately

it's being done. Everyone is just having fun, and sockballs are so soft that no one gets hurt.

To add to the fun, call out different names, changing the target from buns to other body parts. For example, you could say, "Hit the Knee and Flee," or "Hit the Back and Attack," or "Hit the Arm and Do No Harm," or "Hit the Leg, Make 'Em Beg," or "Hit the Fingers If They Linger," or "Hit the Neck and not the Deck."

Or ask the players to come up with their own rhyme.

Schmertz Ball

Roll up a couple of socks and tuck them into the toes of a tube or knee sock. (See illustration.) One by one, have players swing the schmertz ball around their heads, then let go and see how far it goes. Players can throw the ball to each other, or throw it alone and measure the distance thrown each time. Or they can aim at a target and really learn how to direct a schmertz ball.

Sock Weights

Stuff two plastic bags of sand in the toe of a long tube sock. Close the cuff of the sock with a string or with needle and thread and distribute a bag of sand to each

end. Tie a string around each end to keep the sand bag in place. You might want to make two of these socks weights.

Use the weights like barbells and do "reps," or drape them over ankle or thigh for resistive leg lifts. (See illustration.)

It's a good idea to use a plastic bag within another plastic bag, so that if one bag gets ripped, the other one will keep the sand from leaking out.

Dunk Ball

Lay out a variety of targets: a rope coil, a hula hoop, a wastebasket, a dishpan, a bucket, a pot, a coffee can, a shoe, a garden hose coil, an inner tube, a bicycle tire, a rock, a street sign, and a hole dug in the ground. (See illustration.)

Give each player three or more sockballs to use on each turn. The idea is to see how many sockballs you can get in the various targets, just like at a carnival.

Introducing a large variety of targets leads kids into making up throwing games on their own.

The targets can be laid out in a long line so that several kids can play at once. Sometimes it's so hard to "wait your turn."

Target Sockball

All you need is some sockballs and some targets:

- Build a pyramid of aluminum cans and knock them down.

- Line up a row of empty cereal boxes and knock them down one by one, or set them up like dominoes and knock them all down in one fell swoop.

- Build a tower of empty half-gallon milk cartons and knock them down.

- Ask someone whether he would like to be a moving target for the thrower!

Sockball Solitaire

In this game each player gets one sockball and a series of instructions on how to throw it. Some of the instructions are easy to carry out, while others might seem impossible. Don't dwell too long on any one activity—just long enough to give each person the chance to try it. Even the almost impossible ones are fun to try!

Using a sockball, ask your player to:

- Throw low and catch with two hands

- Throw higher and catch with two hands

- Throw very high and catch with two hands

- Repeat the first three using only one hand

- Catch it underhand, first with the right hand, then the left

- Catch it overhand, switching hands

- Throw low and clap once, catching first with two hands, then one

- Throw high and clap twice or three times, then catch with two hands or only one

- Throw the sockball way up, twirl around in a circle, and catch it

- Throw from one hand to another, first with eyes open and then with eyes closed

- Throw it up as always, but wait to catch it until it's four inches from the floor

- Lie down, throw the sockball, stand up, and catch it

- Walk and keep the sockball in the air using just the backs of your hands

- Throw and catch standing on one foot

- Throw and catch with one eye closed or with both eyes closed

- See how far you can throw the sockball

- Put the sockball on your head, then bend your head forward and catch it with your hands

- Put the sockball on your head, then bend your head backward, and catch the sockball behind you

- Bounce the sockball off the wall and catch it

- Bounce the sockball off the wall and clap or twirl around before catching it

- Bounce the sockball off your hip or off your knee and catch it

Bleach Ball

Remove the bottoms from two empty bleach containers or other plastic gallon jugs, leaving the handles on. Holding their jugs upside down, players toss a sockball back and forth, catching and throwing, using only the containers. (See illustration.) You can also use upside-down traffic cones.

Sockball Kicks

Kick a sockball between partners or in a circle of people. Start close together or in a tight circle, and with each successful kick, take a step backward.

Goal Kicks

See how many kicks it takes to go from one goal to another. Put a section of newspaper down to mark one goal and another to mark the end goal. See whether the player can cover the distance with fewer kicks each time.

Socker Ball

Have players dribble a sockball across the room using the insides of their feet. Next, have them try the outsides of their feet. Make sure both the left and right foot are used. If you and your child are doing this together, spend some time passing one sockball back and forth to each other while dribbling it across the room.

Back Race

In this game, each player bends over and places a sock-ball on her back Ready? Race!

One of the advantages of the sockball is that it lies flatter and is less likely to roll than a "real" ball.

Sock Slide

A pair of socks (they don't have to match) and a slick wood or linoleum floor make a challenging balancing combination. Have your player start off at a run and then slide. The object is to stay upright until the end! You probably won't have to even give directions for this game—socks and a slick floor call out to children to do this activity!

As a group game, this can get to resemble a bumper car derby, so if you do it in a group, make sure it's the kind of group that can tolerate spills and falls.

Sockball Path

Lay sockballs of different colors on the floor in a random pattern. See how quickly players can hop or jump from one to the other, picking up the balls along the way. Try

to get them to do it with barely a pause to pick up the ball; see whether they can swoop it up instead.

Variation: Call out the sequence to jump. For example: "Jump first to the lime green ball, then the forest green one, and then the pale blue one."

Sunday Stroll

Players put socks on their hands as if they were elegant gloves and the players were ladies and gentlemen going on a stroll together.

The game is for partners or groups of three to walk side by side without touching but at exactly the same speed. Each person takes a turn being the leader and setting the pace. The leader gets to keep changing the speed of the walk during his or her turn; the others have to stay in step by speeding up or slowing down. They do this not necessarily by looking at the leader but by feeling the movement beside them. Physically experiencing someone else's movements is good for developing empathy, and having others imitate your movements is empowering!

I got this game idea when my daughter Roxanne told me that once, while she and two others were walking together, the three kids discovered that they all walked along at different paces. Randy took long strides, Roxanne took small steps, and Naj was somewhere in the middle. So as they walked along, they

would say, "Let's do Randy's pace," and imitate his rhythm; then they would do Roxanne's rhythm; then Naj's. It was clearly a happy memory for her.

Rhythm Balls

In this game the first person establishes a rhythm sound, such as "be..bop..beeee....." "be..bop..beeee....." On the third or fourth "bop" he or she tosses the sockball to the next player, who repeats the rhythm, also passing the ball on the "bop" sound. The idea is to try and maintain the rhythm while moving the ball back and forth or around the circle. This game can be played as easily with just two people as with a larger group.

Other variations are to use physical movement patterns instead of sound. Hop on the right foot, hop on the left, then throw while jumping on both feet would be one example.

Players can take turns making up new sounds or movements for the others to imitate.

Knee Sock Stretch

Have the player hold a knee sock at either end and stretch it up over his head. Then, still holding both ends, he lowers it behind him and steps over it, brings it up in

front, and does it again. Next time have him go the other way.

If you don't have a sock long enough, tie two together. This is a good exercise for parents to do, too, as we tend to stiffen unless we practice staying flexible.

Sock an Attitude

Add some spice to your ball games and ask your players to throw the ball with an attitude.

Here are two attitude games to play with a group.

- One player is leader and throws the ball as if she were (pick one): mean, cool, tired, scared, secretive, bossy, super-strong, sick, "spacey," and so on. Others in the circle imitate the attitude in their own style.

- Each person has a secret attitude he or she adopts when throwing the ball. Others have to guess what that attitude is.

Sound Catch

Players sit in a circle. The player with the sockball makes a sound and tosses the ball to another player, who

catches it, quickly makes another sound, and throws the ball to the next person. Ask the players not to try and think of a sound but just to let it come from within. There are no right sounds or wrong sounds; any sound is perfectly okay. Spontaneity, speed, and keeping the rhythm are the goals, along with catching the ball, of course.

Once the rhythm and speed are comfortable, think of things to call out instead of just making sounds—things like names of colors, friends, states, trees, flowers, actors, teachers, rock singers, songs, and so on.

Hot Sock/Cold Sock

Form a circle and toss the sockball around from person to person. One person gets to be Caller. When the Caller calls out "Hot Sock," the players toss the sockball overhand to each other as quickly as possible; when she says "Cold Sock," the players toss it gently and slowly underhand until the next command is given.

Variations: If the group is older, add "Goofball" to the repertoire. Players lift one leg and toss the sockball under it to another player. Other possibilities include:

- Twirly Ball: After catching the sockball, the player has to twirl around before throwing it. There could be a Hot Twirly Ball and a Cold Twirly Ball.

- Sound Ball: The thrower has to make a silly sound before throwing the sockball. Advanced players could have calls like Hot Twirly Sound Ball, in which the players try to catch the ball, twirl around, make a sound, and throw it quickly overhand!

The same game can be played sitting down if there is a problem with balancing and catching at the same time. Variations when sitting include:

- Open Scissors: Legs have to be open in a "V" shape

- Closed Scissors: Legs closed and straight

- Tailor Style: Legs crossed (You could elaborate with Tailor Style Right, which means right leg crossed in front, or Tailor Style Left, with left leg in front. This can make for some interesting movements during the game, when the caller switches quickly from one tailor style to another and back again.)

- One-Hand Catch: One hand behind your back while catching with the other (Again, there could be Right Hand Back and Left Hand Back.)

Ask the players to come up with other ideas. One player came up with the idea for Teeth Catch: The sock-ball had to be caught and thrown from the teeth. It wasn't a very accurate way to go about catching and throwing, but it sure got everyone to focus!

Human Pinball

The group stands in a circle facing outward, with one person in the center. Players bend over and shoot sockballs between their legs to try and hit the player in the center, who is allowed to dodge as much as he likes. The first person to hit the target player is the next to stand in the center.

Shield Ball

The group stands in two concentric circles, with the outside circle facing inward and a few people in the center forming an inner circle facing outward. Each center person holds a shield (one side of a cardboard box). The people on the outside of the circle try to hit people in the inside with the sockballs (see illustration), while those people on the inside try to protect themselves by deflecting the balls with their shields. When hit, the shield bearer trades places with the sock thrower, giving over her shield. If she doesn't know whence came the ball that struck her, she just throws down her shield, and moves to the outside of the circle, and the sock thrower goes inside and picks up the shield. Several sockballs are used to ensure that the game moves quickly and that everyone gets to be inside the circle many times.

Be prepared for a bit of chaos as balls go flying, shields are dropped, and kids run back and forth, trading places.

I did this game with my younger daughter's class when she was in elementary school. The teacher was uncomfortable with the wildness and changed the rules so that everyone waited quietly for a "1-2-3- throw" command before each throw. I had to admire the new orderliness of the game, but as my daughter pointed out later, it lost a lot of the fun.

Caboose Ball

This game is played like Shield Ball, except that the three or four players in the middle form a small train. The engine is the only person who holds a shield, and the only legal place to hit the train is the caboose end of the caboose—so it is up to the engine of the line to move the train around to protect the rear as much as possible.

When the caboose is hit, that person becomes the engine and the next person in line becomes the new caboose, When everyone in the train line has had a turn being the caboose and the engine, a new group of players becomes the next train.

Dragon Tail

Players stand in line, each holding on to the waist of the person in front. A knee sock dangles loosely from the belt or the waist of the pants of the last person in line. At the signal, the dragon begins to chase his tail! The first person in line tries to grab the sock while everyone holds on for the chase.

Players in dresses or without waistbands or belts can make a belt by tying a few socks together and tucking the sock tail into the sock belt.

Sock Tail Tag

Everyone has a sock dangling from the back of his or her pants. (If someone has a dress on, tie a few socks together to make a belt and hang the sock from that.) At the signal, the players all run around and try to take the others' socks, holding on to them until the end of the game. The game ends

when everyone's sock has been taken. At this point anyone who has stolen socks in her hands throws them into the air, everyone grabs one and tucks an end into the back of his pants or belt, and the game begins again.

Go Fish

This is played just like the card game, except with single socks instead of cards. This is the game to play before making sockballs to see whether any of the socks in your collection should be married and put in the sock drawer, or whether they are all truly unmatched singles.

Deal out a "hand" of six socks to each player; the rest go in a bag. One player says, "Anyone have a green sock with blue hearts on it?" The others either give up the mate or tell the player to "go fish" in the bag. All the socks left divorced, widowed, or otherwise unmated are made into sockballs.

Sock Knee Pads

This one is not exactly a game—more like a household tip. If you have a very young child just learning to crawl, discarded socks make great kneepads. Your little one may be more willing to brave the hard floors with a little extra cushioning on her knees.

Take a sock and cut the appropriate amount from the top. The thicker the sock, the better the reinforcement. Make sure you use socks with tight weaves, so they won't stretch out quickly or come off while crawling.

Sock Puppets

Stuff a sock with cotton, scrap material or other socks and draw a face on the toe with felt-tip markers. Or, if your learner is able, have him sew buttons for eyes and yarn for hair. Make a few of these puppets and put on a show!

Games to play with lids

Lids are what's left over after you've recycled your glass jars and bottles. Lids are those nice plastic tops that come with coffee cans and margarine tubs, and somehow hang around long after their bottoms have been discarded. Lids are those apparently useless things that cover yogurt and cottage cheese containers, and can't be recycled. Lids are also bottle caps, and bottle caps have always found their way into kids' pockets. Now here are some reasons for us to save these lids: games!

Lid Jump

This one takes coordination on the part of the adult present. The player jumps up with legs apart, and the adult throws the lid between his legs.

Once the player gets the idea, try throwing first and having your learner jump at just the right moment.

Large Lid Jump

Roll the large plastic lid from a five-gallon bucket across the floor toward the player. Her job, as in "Lid Jump," is to jump over it as it comes her way. Except that this time she needs to jump a little higher!

Matching Lids

Place a wide variety of jars with lids in front of your learner. Take all the lids off and toss them together, mixing them all up. Then see how quickly your player can put the right lids on the right jars.

Lid Sliders

Use metal bottle caps (harder to find nowadays because of pop top cans) or the plastic caps from mineral water bottles.

Two contestants sit across from each other at a flat, smooth table and play these Lid Slider variations.

- Slide a cap back and forth to each other

- Use two caps and slide to each other at the same time

- Slide caps toward each other, trying to get them to collide in the middle

- Make "goal posts" at either end out of two caps and have the players try to slide their cap through the posts

- Make a line of caps and have the players try to hit each cap and knock it out of line

- Make a line of caps (pennies work well for this also) with at least an inch of space between them, and have the players slide their caps through each of the spaces in turn (It's a good idea to make the first space the largest, with each of the following spaces progressively smaller.)

Have the players try "flicking" the caps instead of sliding them, using the thumb and middle finger.

Lid Pictures

Use a plastic lid such as the kind that comes with coffee cans. Punch holes in the top using a hole puncher or pencil (your job!), thread some embroidery thread on a large darning needle, and have your worker go in and out of the holes, making a colorful design or picture on the lid. How complicated you make this project depends on your child's level.

Lid Roll

Show your child how to place a lid on its edge, give it a little push, and watch it roll. A lid can be rolled at a target or simply to see how far it can go without falling over.
Try rolling a lid in each hand at the same time.

Flying Saucers and Other Games

Both plastic and metal lids can be used for throwing.

- Use them like frisbees

- See how high they can be thrown, or how far

- Try for accuracy; make a target to throw at

- Try to throw straight, or in a curve

When Lids Collide

Have your child throw something up in the air with one hand (a soda pop can, a yogurt container, a newspaper ball) and then try and hit it with a lid with the other hand. (See illustration.)

Lid Catch

Have your child hold a lid in each hand, toss something in the air (a newspaper ball, an aluminum can, an ice cream or yogurt container), and catch it between the two lids.

To increase the challenge, have the player walk while catching.

Lid Flip

Place some lids on the floor with their containers on top of them—yogurt containers work well—and have your player flip the lid with his toe, ejecting the container. Lay out a series of these and see how quickly he can flip the containers off the lids. (See illustration.)

Double Lids

In this game, the player kicks a lid so that it hits a second lid. (See illustration.)

Lid Skating

Players stand on large lids and scoot and skate their way forward.

Lid Balance

How many lids can your children balance on his head while walking? Start with one, keep walking, and add another, and another, and another.

Lid Shakers

To make a lid shaker, tape two lids together after filling one with rice or beans or pennies or shells or whatever will make a noise when shaken. Give one lid shaker to your learner and keep one for yourself; then ask her or them to copy your rhythm. Start with a simple one/two beat and work up.

If, for example, you are asking her to copy you shaking your lids three beats in a row before a pause, change where the emphasis is. Put it on the first beat, then the middle, then the last. Make this activity as simple or as complicated as you need.

Lid Touch

In this game all the players except the one who is "It" are scattered around the room. "It" starts kicking a lid around on the floor; whoever it touches becomes "It" and takes over the kicking of the lid.

Variation: When the lid touches someone's foot, instead of replacing the original "It," that person becomes a second "It," taking another lid and kicking it (scooting it, really) until someone else is touched. Then there are three "Its." This continues until everyone has a lid.

This naturally segues into . . .

Lid Race

Starting in a line at one end of the room, the players see who can kick or dribble their lid to the other end the fastest without losing control of it.

Lid Kicks

Standing side by side in a line, players take turns seeing how far they can kick their lids. In the first round use the right foot; in the second, the left. Players can see which is their more accurate leg.

CHAPTER ELEVEN

Games to play with wood

These games require easy-to-find wooden objects such as clothespins, toothpicks, doweling, chairs, tables, two-by-fours, broomsticks, and left-over scraps from the lumber mill.

Obstacle Course

You can make elaborate obstacle courses using ordinary household furniture, plus a balance beam, if you have one. Turn to page *212* to find out how to make your own balance beam. Make up a story to go along with the course.

Example: "One day, Janie set out to look for frogs. First she had to go over a high mountain (climb up and over a desk or table). Then she had to jump over a river (coat lying on floor), squeeze under a fence (go under a desk or table), and find her way through a deep forest (two uneven rows of chairs that the child must weave through, slalom-style). At last she came to a bridge, where she found the frogs sunning themselves. Janie crossed the bridge, picking the frogs up as she went along. (Sockballs make good frogs—or you can use imaginary frogs.) Then she went home: across the bridge, through the forest, under the fence, over the river, and back over the mountain again!"

Chair Push

This game requires a smooth floor and a weighted chair. The learner's job is to push the weighted chair from one

point to another. The weight on the chair can be anything from a box of books to another child, and the path can be a straight line or a curved one marked on the floor with masking tape. There could also be musical accompaniment to cue the learner when to stop and start.

Chair Step

How about a homemade stairmaster? Have your child step up on a chair and then step down again, repeating this motion over and over. Whether you use a stool, a low chair, or a regular-size chair depends on the child's strength and size. See how many times he can get up and down in one or more minutes.

Classroom Games

If you are a parent volunteering in a classroom and find that the children need five minutes of movement after a long period of sitting, try these classroom games. Clear off all desk areas and have children:

- Lie on their desks on their backs and spin around like break dancers
- Kneel on chairs and place hands flat on their desks and do push ups

- Step from floor to chair to desk and back down again as many times as they can in one minute

- Walk around the room weaving in and out of the desks and chairs without touching any of them

Furniture Walk

Set up a path of sturdy furniture for your player to walk on. Make some of the gaps between objects fairly wide so your player can stretch her balancing skills. Of course, you'll need to be there with a helping hand, if needed.

Under-Chair Kick

Place a chair right side up and have the player kick something—a ball, a can, a newspaper ball—under the bottom rungs of the chair and between the legs. Make a path of chairs for the player to kick the ball under, moving it from one chair to the next.

Change the position of the chair(s) to change the size and shape of the pathway.

Chair Tunnel

Overturn some sturdy wooden chairs so they form a
tunnel for your player to crawl through. Have a reward
at the end of the tunnel—anything from some Cheerios to
a big hug!

Chair Path

Place two rows of chairs back to back with a large aisle
between them. Ask your player to walk between the
chairs without touching them. Keep reducing the distance
between the chairs so the child finally has to walk sideways on toes to get through without touching them.

Chair Walk

Place a line of sturdy chairs in a path and have players
walk from seat to seat, jumping off the last chair.

Chair Train

Line up a row of chairs front to back and tell the children
they are going on a train ride. One person gets to be the

conductor and punch holes in everyone's pretend or real tickets. (Take turns if necessary.) Children bounce around in unison as the train "moves," while you encourage them to talk about what they are seeing out the "windows."

Non-Competitive Musical Chairs

In case you don't know this version of Musical Chairs, it's played just like the original: Children run around a line of chairs while the music is playing and make a dash for a seat when it stops. Each time the music stops, a chair is removed, so that there is one fewer chair each round. The difference is that instead of taking the child who can't get a seat out of the game, you leave all the children in the game, explaining that they have to share the remaining seats. By the end, all the children are piled onto one chair. As you can see, this is a people-friendly game.

Variation: Go back to the original version of the game, in which a child is removed, except that instead of making the removed child sit on the sidelines, invite her to join the band! You start off the game with just one child singing while the others run around. The singer gets to decide when to stop singing and make the others scramble for a chair. One by one, the left-out children then join the singing group, with the first singer becoming the conductor and directing when the group starts and stops each song.

LADDER GAMES
Go in and out the Window

Although a ladder might not be your usual re-cyclable item, broken ones that are no longer safe to be used as ladders can make effective props for games. Of course, you can use a perfectly good ladder just as well. One game is to prop the ladder on its side. The players start at one end and crawl in and out the spaces between the rungs, weaving their way down to the other end. (See illustration.)

I like to sing an old children's song as the children crawl through the ladder: "Go in and out the window, go in and out the window, go in and out the window, all on a lovely day."

Ladder Games

As stated in the idea above, a ladder no longer useful as a ladder can make a nice piece of equipment for games. Lay the ladder flat on the floor and have the player

- Walk on the rungs from one end to the other

- Walk in the spaces

- Walk on the sides of the ladder

Or prop up one or both ends of the ladder using something sturdy like concrete building blocks and do the same activities

Ladder Lift

Have the group lift up a ladder and tilt it so that one person can climb on. The group then carries this person across the room and tilts the ladder so she can climb down again. This game encourages group strength and trust.

If carrying the ladder and passenger is more than the group can manage, have them simply tilt the ladder, let one person go across, tilt the ladder the opposite way, and let the person off.

BOARDS AND BEAMS
Walk the Plank

If your little one is not quite ready for balance beam games, start with this game and the next one, "Straddle Walk." Place two two-by-fours on the floor three feet apart and have your player walk between

them. Then continue to narrow the distance between the boards on each successive turn until the player is doing a heel-to-toe walk. (See illustration.)

Straddle Walk

Lay a single two-by-four on the floor and ask your player to walk with one foot on each side of it, consciously shifting his weight from one foot to the other as he walks.

Making a Balance Board

The balance board I use is a square platform measuring sixteen by sixteen inches, which is nailed on a three-inch-high balance post. (See illustration.) Three sizes (thicknesses) of balance post may be used: three by three, four by four, and five by five. The boards with the larger balance posts are the easiest to balance. Gluing rubber or a carpet square to the top surface of the board prevents feet from slipping off.

Games to play on a Balance Board

1. Sit or stand on the board, depending on your skill level, and throw objects such as bean bags into a bucket or other container.

2. Bounce the ball around yourself.

3. Blow and break bubbles.

4. Move your hips to music.

5. Standing with your feet close together and your arms extended and parallel, pivot at the hip and from side to side. Also try swinging your arms, rocking back and forth from heels to toes, and anything else that encourages a shift in balance.

6. Suspend a ball in front of the board at eye level to swat at.

7. Have someone else on another balance board, and suspend a ball between the two so they can bat it back and forth to each other.

Making a Balance Beam

The balance beam is a two-by-four measuring eight to twelve feet in length. Each end is fitted into a wooden

bracket that serves as a brace and prevents the board from tipping over; when assembled, the board is raised approximately two inches off the floor. Each bracket has a combination fitting, so that the board can be set flat with the wide surface up or on its edge with the narrow surface up. Beginners can use the four-inch surface; then as they become more adept, the board is turned on edge and the two-inch surface used. For the child having extreme difficulty, a two-by-six can be substituted.

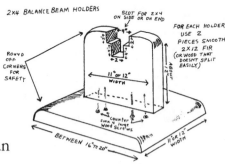

See the diagram for a plan of the bracket.

Two-by-fours can also be propped up off the ground with concrete blocks, bricks, or tires. (Tires can add a challenging bounce.)

Games to Play on the Balance Beam

1. Start a young child on a beam on the floor, not propped up, or use two balance beams side by side to walk across or between. If you only have one beam, have the young player put one foot on the beam and the other on the floor and walk along that way. It's a silly, fun, and unscary way to cross a beam the first time.

2. Encourage your child to look straight ahead rather than down at the beam by asking her to focus on something at eye level. That something could be you, a mirror you hold up, a picture, or a series of signs, like the old Burma shave road signs.

3. Children have fun pretending that the beam is a bridge over dangerous water; they have to carry something across. That something could be a tray with a stack of empty cracker boxes on it; each time the bridge is crossed, one more box is added to the tray. Or the tray could hold a plastic glass of water, each glassful to be emptied into a bucket at the end. Other possibilities: peanuts on a spoon; oranges on outstretched palms.

4. Try having your child pick up small objects that are scattered along the beam: beanbags, poker chips, a trail of peanuts. . .

5. Two children could walk sideways across the beam together. Or a whole line of children could cross together holding on to each other's waist.

6. Try different ways to cross a balance beam. Going forward, for example, you can have one foot lead, while the other follows in a sort of shuffle step or you can alternate feet in a regular walking pattern.

Crossing sideways, you can have the same foot lead each step or do a cross-over step. One foot crossing over the other to take turns leading.

Going backward it's the same thing: One can lead in that shuffle-backward pattern or you can alternate feet. Start beginners with the first possibility.

Can players come up with other ways to step?

7. Walk with one eye closed; then try both eyes closed.

8. Walk to the middle, do a 360-degree turn, and come back to the start. Do the same move on the sideways and backward walks.

9. Walk on heels only or toes only.

10. Walk to the middle, turn around, and return to the start.

11. Walk in a squatting position.

12. Walk in tiny steps (toe/heel pattern) or taking big strides.

13. Walk with bean bags on your head, on your out-stretched palms, or on the backs of your hands.

14. Wear only one shoe, or high-heeled shoes, or only one high-heeled shoe, or no shoes!

15. Carry two buckets of water to be emptied into a container at the end of the beam. (A good *outdoor* summer game.)

16. Put your hands on your head, on your hips, folded, in your pocket, or folded behind your back.

17. Keep a balloon in the air with your hands while walking across.

18. Dribble a ball on the floor while walking across.

19. Walk in a toe/heel fashion, with your heel touching the toe of the other foot as you walk forward or backward.

20. Walk in a cross-over fashion, with one leg crossing over the other leg with each step; sometimes the leg crosses in front, sometimes behind.

21. Two players walk forward from opposite ends of the beam and try to pass each other without either one falling off.

22. Roll a pair of dice and cross the beam the number of times the dice dictate.

23. Hold a hula hoop or circle made from plumbing pipe over the beam and have the player go through the hoop.

24. Hold a bar over the beam for the player to step over as she crosses.

25. Hold a hoop or bar over the beam and move it up and down in a steady rhythm so that the player has to time his movement and go over the bar or through the hoop when it is in the down position.

Going to the Store

This game needs a balance beam and a lot of empty grocery store items, such as cereal boxes, margarine containers, cracker boxes, milk cartons, peanut cans, salt boxes, and so on. The adult plays the mother or father, the players are her the children, and the balance beam plays a bridge.

The children and the parent are at one end of the bridge and a table with all the grocery items on it is at the other end. Each child is given instructions by the parent as to what item to get at the grocery store. How the items are requested depends on the skill level of the player. For example, the parent might say, "Bring me something that

- . . . is yellow." (Or any other color that's appropriate.)

- . . . starts with the letter M." (Or the sound Mmmmmm, or any other letter or sound that is appropriate.)

- . . . is big." (Or small)

- . . . there are two of." (Or three of. Provide a tray for carrying, if needed.)

- . . . goes with milk." Or you put on toast, or other "goes with" ideas.)

- . . . you would eat for breakfast." (Or lunch, dinner, or snack.)

The instructions as to how the child should cross the "bridge" to get to the store also depend on the skill level of the child. Possibilities include:

- Cross forward

- Cross sideways

- Cross backward

- Cross forward on the way to the store and backward on the way home

- Cross backward on the way to the store and with your eyes closed on the way home.

- Cover your left eye on the way to the store and your right on the way home.

- Two players cross together holding a tray, one walking backward and one forward.

A major benefit of this game is that the group can include a wide range of ages and skills. Each child can

play on her own level and still be very much a part of the group!

Feel and Cross

As in "Going to the Store," the players cross the beam to get something from a table on the other side. This time, however, they are looking for an object that matches one they felt.

Collect a large variety of items, making sure you have two of each. Things like spoons, pencils, paper clips, paperback books, combs, hairbrushes, forks, bowls, material scraps, and erasers all work well. Then divide the objects into two matching sets, arranging one set on the table and placing the second set in a bag.

The player whose turn it is stands on one end of the beam and put his hands behind his back. You place an item from your bag into his hands and ask him to feel it without looking at it. When he is done feeling, remove the item and ask him to cross the beam and find a similar item on the table. Once he finds it, he can either hold up the item for everyone to see or bring it back across the beam with him.

Again, if you wish, you can suggest various ways to cross the beam (backward, sideways, eyes closed, and so on) to get in some more work on balance and remembering sequences.

Balance Beam Variations

- Remove the bracket from one end of the beam so that it forms a ramp. The players can now walk up the ramp and jump off the high end. Have them try it backward, sideways, or with eyes closed; or, starting from the high end of the ramp, have them run down to the low end.

- Put one bracket in the middle of the beam for a "see-saw" effect—and a challenging walk across!

- Use two balance beams set up at different levels and have the player cross them with a foot on each beam. (The game is good for increasing one's awareness of being a two-sided person.)

- Have the players stand beside the beam and jump over it, or stand far away from the beam and then run and jump over it.

- To promote synchronized rhythm, have two or more children do the running and jumping together. Remind them to be aware of each other and to try and jump at the same time, rather than having one person drag the other along.

- Have players squiggle under the beam in a prone position (face down) and then in a supine one (face up).

Making a Belly Board

For a belly board, I use a piece of plywood
twelve inches wide, eighteen inches long, and approximately one inch thick. The board can be
made smaller to accommodate smaller children. A
two-inch ball bearing plate caster is screwed to each
corner of the underside of the board about two
inches in from the edge. Midway along each of the
four sides of the board, a hole is drilled about one inch
from the edge. A rope can be tied through the front or
back hole for pulling the board, and cloth ties can be
threaded through the side holes for "seat belts."

Sit and Ride

In this game, a child simply sits on the belly board,
strapped in with "seat belt" if needed, and is pulled around
the room. Make unpredictable zigs and zags in the path,
including jiggling the board. Or let another child pull.

Zoom and Pick-Up

Propelling a belly board along with one's hands while
lying on it face down is a fast way to get around a room.

To control the speed, add little tasks, such as, "How many dominoes can you pick up between here and there in two minutes?"

Rope Pull-Along

Tie a rope to a stationary object. Players sit on a belly board and pull themselves along from one end of the rope to the other.

Sitting Walk

The rider sits on a board and pulls herself along using her legs and feet in a walking pattern. Make a path on the floor with masking tape or ropes for her to follow. As she gets more capable, give the path curves or zigzags to increase the challenge.

Beginning Skateboarding

Children who aspire to riding a real skateboard someday or who just want to pretend they're riding one already love standing on a belly board and being pulled around the room, gently.

Skate Along

Somewhat more advanced players can push themselves along skateboard style, with one foot on the board and the other foot propelling it.

It's even possible to get the board to twirl around in circles, if one is so inclined.

BROOMSTICK GAMES
Broomstick Jump

Place a broomstick or long dowel across two chairs spaced far enough apart for a player to run through them, jumping over the stick.

Make sure that the backs of the chairs face the runner, so that if he hits the stick with his foot, it will roll off the chair and not trip him.

Broomstick Limbo

Have two children hold the ends of a broomstick so that it is parallel to the ground. The rest of the children get in a line and go under the stick by bending their bodies backward while jumping their feet forward. The stick con-

tinues to get lower for each turn, until the only way to get under it without touching it is to slither on one's back.

Broomstick Stepping

Holding a broomstick in both hands, the player steps over it so that it is behind him, then steps back over so it is in front.

Then he brings the stick up and over his head and behind his back and legs, steps over it, and ends with the broomstick in front of him again.

Broomstick Ride

Play pretend. Turn the broomstick into a horse and gallop away. Or be a witch and fly. Or hold it in front and have it be the restraining bar of a roller coaster ride.

Encourage your player to come up with other ideas.

Broomstick Drop

This game moves quickly! Players form a circle, with the person in the middle holding a broomstick or long dowel. The center person calls out the name of one of the other players, then lets go of the broomstick and joins the circle. The person whose name was called runs to the center and tries to grab the broomstick before it hits the ground. Then, he names someone else to catch it.

To make the challenge equal for all players, the circle (or it could be a square) can be marked with a rope so that everyone is the same distance away.

The bigger the circle, the bigger the challenge. Start small.

Broomstick Sway

Everyone holds on to the broomstick, and one person starts to sway. setting up a rhythm. All go with the motion. This can be a very relaxing activity, making everyone feel part of the whole. However, different players should have a turn changing the rhythm to their own particular tune.

TOOTHPICKS AND OTHER ODDS AND ENDS

Toothpick Designs

In this game you and your player each have a set of toothpicks to work with. Take turns making designs for the other person to copy, alternating between pictorial images, such as faces or people, and abstract patterns.

Toothpick Cake

This game is for little ones just learning to put pegs in pegholes. It requires a piece of clay or a styrofoam block, the kind used for packing; or, if you are outside, a mound of damp dirt will do just fine. That's right, this is the cake. Does it look good enough to eat?

Have your learner put toothpick "candles" into the cake, making a lot of little holes. After you sing "Happy Birthday" together and blow out the candles, remove them. Now comes the tricky part: Ask your player to put the toothpicks back in the same holes. Later, slice and "eat" the cake!

You can also play this game using nails, sticks, or pieces of doweling.

Toothpick Sculptures

Combine cut-up toothpicks and whole raisins to make abstract sculptures or models of animals. You can also use softened dried peas instead of raisins. (See illustration.)

Toothpick Throw

Picking up tiny toothpicks and throwing them into a container is a fun and simple activity.

Dowel Balance

Have your child hold a dowel in either hand and balance a third on top of them. Have him try walking while balancing the third dowel, or flipping it and catching it with the other two. (See illustration.)

Rings and Things

Stick a piece of dowel in a lump of clay, floral sponge, can of sand, or anything to keep it upright. The game is to put things on the dowel stick. Beginners can start with canning rings or circles made out of cardboard.

I cut up a milk carton and use the sides for stiff paper, then cut holes of different sizes in them. The smaller the hole, the harder the game;, I make a variety of sizes.

You could also make a dowel series by starting with a one-inch-diameter dowel and going down to a quarter-incher. The rings then could range from round plastic bracelets to small washers.

Musical Dowels

Cut up pieces of doweling for rhythm sticks and give each player a pair to bang together. Play around with the different sounds that come from hitting the sticks together softly and with more vigor. Have one person make up a rhythm for another person to dance to.

Cup Hook Challenge

Screw cup hooks into a piece of wood and give your learner some washers or bread wrapper tabs to put on each hook. For a more complicated activity, you can use tabs of different colors or different sizes of washers, and ask the child to sort them accordingly: All the red tabs on one hook, all the blue on another, or by size and so on.

Wood Collage

Ask a cabinet maker or industrial arts teacher for lathed scraps, planning curls, button molds, wood scraps and sawdust. Then let your learner either make a collage or a sculpture out of them using Elmer's or wood glue.

Wood Instruments

Get small pieces of flat wood (check with furniture makers' shops or lumber yards), and attach a knob or smaller piece of wood to one side of each for something to hold on to. Use the pieces like "Musical Dowels," or add sandpaper to the flat bottoms and make a neat sound by rubbing them together.

Clothespin Pick-up

Exercise the small muscles of your feet! Take turns picking up clothespins with your toes and dropping them into a bucket.

Better yet, challenge your youngsters to pick up their dirty laundry off the floor and put it in a laundry basket. Play this foot game and clean a room at the same time!

Clothespin Drop

Have your player drop clothespins into a container. The variables are the choice of container and the height of the drop. Easiest would be dropping them into a coffee can from a kneeling position. Hardest would be dropping them into an open-spouted milk carton while standing on a chair. Other container possibilities: a plastic shampoo bottle, a yogurt container, a paper cup, a toilet paper roll, a metal juice can. . .

Clothespin Throw

Make a target, such as a laid-out piece of rope or a waste-basket, and have your worker throw the clothespins to the rope or into the basket.

Clothespin Slip

Take some of those old fashioned clothespins with the slit up the middle and slip them over the sides of a can. Ask your little one to take them off the sides and drop them inside the can, then take them out and slip them back onto the side

Stepping Block

Lumber yards and construction sites sometimes have "mill ends," which are the cut-off ends of two-by-fours. These make nice blocks for games, especially stepping stone games. Lay the blocks out in a path on the floor and have the players step from block to block trying not to fall into the "water." Children's wooden building blocks can be used for this game, too.

Tongue Depressor or Popsicle Stick Puzzles

Tape popsicle sticks or tongue depressors together as if making a raft. Draw a simple bold design or picture on one side using felt-tip markers; then untape the sticks and give the pieces to your learner to put together. Or have her make and draw her own puzzle for you to put together.

Games to play with other ordinary things

This chapter is devoted to all those other miscellaneous items, like bubble wrap and styrofoam blocks and old bicycle tires and torn sheets—things that are around and can be used and reused for games. There must be an infinite variety of games out there to be discovered, many more than are included here. I hope these ideas will inspire you to think of them.

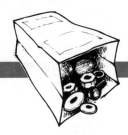

Bubble Wrap Jump

You know bubble wrap—that plastic packing material made of rows of bubbles. Even adults find it hard to resist squeezing those bubbles, they make such a satisfying "pop!" when they burst. They make an even better noise when you jump on them, and jumping off a chair onto a sheet of bubble wrap is so inviting to children that even the most timid are willing to try.

Bicycle Tire Games

Used bicycle tires, which can be had free from bicycle shops, can be used in most of the hoop games listed in chapter 4.

Inner Tube Bounce

A used truck tire inner tube, which can be obtained from a tire store, provides endless mileage. (Sorry!) For example, have your player bounce on one while sitting, kneeling, or standing.

Or have him jump in and out of it.

Or place it on a mat so that children can bounce on one side, spring to the other side, and finally land inside the tire.

Remember to be sure the air intake valve is pointing downward; you may even want to tape it down with duct or strapping tape to make sure the game stays all giggles.

Book Jumps

Librarians will hate me for this, but new jumpers do well jumping off books. Have them work their way up from ordinary textbooks to encyclopedias and mammoth dictionaries.

Carpet Squares

These games use those small carpet samples you see in stores that sell flooring. Go to one and ask whether they have any samples to give away. Carpets, like clothes, go in and out of style; when the new styles come in, the old samples are either given away or sold inexpensively. Stores that install carpets may also can have leftovers you can cut into squares.

Look in chapter 8, "Games to Play with Cardboard Boxes," for any games calling for paper or cardboard

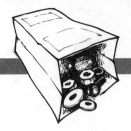

squares. Carpet squares can be used in most of these games, and will hold up better and longer than paper or cardboard.

They also make interesting flying saucers! How far can you throw one?

Punching Bag

An old laundry or duffel bag can be stuffed with newspaper or old clothes and used for a full-body punching bag.

Blanket Pull

If you have a sturdy old blanket, have one child sit on it while another pulls her along the floor. The puller gains strength, and pullee gets to work on her upper trunk balance. If you are the puller (and you're getting stronger every day, like it or not), purposely jiggle the blanket this way and that to give the child extra balancing practice.

Bucket Lift

As a way of strengthening legs, have your worker sit in a chair and lift a bucket with his legs, moving it from one spot to another. Add a beanbag to the bucket and ask him to dump it out at the second spot using only his legs and feet.

Keep increasing the number of bean-bags in the bucket.

Styrofoam Skates

Here is a use for those styrofoam trays that come with meat, besides making bathtub boats. This one is simple enough. Children put a foot on each tray and pretend they are skating away. Lay out a group of obstacles to skate around; or, if you have
more than two kids, hold skating races. I am not big on competitive sports, myself, so when I do racing games, I rarely announce who won but go right on to the next game. The point and fun of racing, I figure, is to be inspired to go faster, not to win over others.

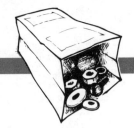

Telephone Wire Shapes

You can get scraps of colorful wire from telephone companies and use them to form different shapes. Make one into a dog, another into a child, then do a puppet show and have the dog and child talk to each other.

Or put the shapes into a soap and water solution that has a bit of oil and food coloring in it, and form colorful and interesting bubbles.

Wallpaper Collage

It's possible to get out-of-date books of wallpaper samples from appropriate stores and to use the varieties of textures and colors and designs they contain to make lovely collages. Tearing the shapes emphasizes increasing finger strength, while cutting them increases fine motor coordination.

Paste the paper on cardboard or use those styrofoam trays meat comes in. They make an instant frame.

Mosaic Tile Collage

Tile stores will give you broken tile that can be used to make interesting collages when glued to a thin piece of

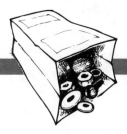

board. Glue them as is, or cut them with special tile cutters to make exact patterns.

Miscellaneous Collage

Gather up a bunch of things, like feathers, buttons, fabric, dry moss, foil, rickrack, bobby pins, sequins, macaroni, pipe cleaners, glitter, toothpicks, and yarn, and show your child how to glue them onto cardboard or styrofoam trays.

Edible Collage

Well, edible—not necessarily delicious. Glue seeds of various kinds, dried peas, corn, beans, and noodles. Or make a collage that's actually tasty and use popcorn, sunflower seeds, and pumpkin seeds. Eat a little, glue a little. You could use eatable glue too, also known as powdered sugar icing, but that might taste odd with shelled sunflower seeds. Then again, it depends on the taster.

Cotton and Tongs

Make a pile of cotton balls and ask your little honey to use a pair of tongs to transfer the balls across the room

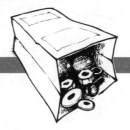

one by one to make another pile. See whether she can pick up other small objects like peanuts and fabric swatches.

Nail Tangle

Bend a couple of used nails around each other in such a way that by manipulating the nails, it is possible to separate them again. Then see whether your child can do it.

Shishkebab Skewer Pick-up

You know the game of pick-up sticks don't you? It's a great game to get kids to increase dexterity and ability to quietly focus their attention. Shishkabab skewers make great pick-up sticks, and they're made from wood, not plastic. An environmental plus!

Wrist Twist

Take some bailing wire or hanger wire and bend it at right angles several times. Attach the two ends of the wire to a file cabinet handle and put a washer on the wire. The activity is to get the washer from one end of the wire to the other.

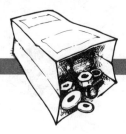

Rubbings

Rubbings are a good way to encourage small hand muscles. They work like this. Take an object like a coin and place a piece of paper over it. Then rub the flat side of a crayon back and forth on the paper directly over the coin, and like magic the drawing on the coin will appear. Almost anything with a texture can be rubbed. The Japanese do rubbings of fish!

Odd Painting

Painting is a good fine-motor activity, and you don't always have to use a brush. Other kinds of "paintbrushes" may be more appropriate for your worker: Try sponges, cotton balls, eyedroppers, powder puffs, toothbrushes, shoe brushes, Q-tips, and corks.

Why stick to paper? Burlap, for that matter, wood, cardboard, grocery bags, and rocks all make good painting surfaces.

Making paintings while blindfolded can be a fun alternative, and sometimes the painting comes out better!

Finally, don't miss putting a blob of paint on the paper and blowing on it—or at it—with a straw. It splatters the paint in an interesting way and exercises lung capacity.

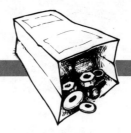

Eyedropper Art

Using an eyedropper filled with paint or ink encourages not only small finger movement but also cognition as the child figures out how to fill the dropper up and control the moment when it drips out. Ideas for eyedropper art include:

- Release a few drops of ink or paint just above the paper. Continue releasing it from progressively higher distances and notice the difference in the results.

- Drop a few drops of different colors and then fold the paper in half for a Rorschach effect.

- Drop a big drop of one color and then speckle it with little drops of another color.

- Drop paint on different surfaces, such as dry, wet, or damp paper, or wax paper or aluminum foil. What are the different effects?

- Drop puddles of paint on the paper and then tip it in various directions.

Food color diluted with water or with a vinegar, water, and oil mix also makes good eyedropper paint.

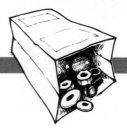

Egg Carton Throw

Mary, a parent of one of my clients, came up with this idea when I lamented that there wasn't much to be done with egg cartons except make those egg carton caterpillars or use them for sorting games. She suggested that kids use a pebble or other small object and throw it into the depressions from varying distances. For a greater challenge, draw a number in each one with a felt-tipped pen and ask kids to aim for a specific cup.

Chalk Games

Chalk will sometimes inspire children because it feels so nice in the hand. Many enjoy making chalk drawings on the sidewalk, and when chalk is scraped into water and a white piece of paper laid on it, it makes lovely patterned stationary. Use real chalk for this one, not a dust-free substitute.

Hair Curlers

Garage sales always seem to have at least one box of hair curlers that lost out to the blow dryer. Often these curlers have interlocking parts or hair clips that can be clipped

on. I like give them to children to mess with while I am getting the next activity ready. They are especially good for people with a weak grip.

Banded Box

Another good busy activity is to give a child a box with a rubber band around it. Sometimes taking a rubber band off a box is just the perfect challenge for small fingers. Have a treat or interesting toy inside as a reward for hard work.

Bandage Hide

Bandage boxes, with their little hinged tops, make a nice manipulative game when children have to open them to find the hidden present inside.

Film Canisters

Free from any camera or film store, film canisters are a level up from bandage boxes because the tops are a little harder to pull off.

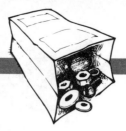

Velcro Finger Pull

Increase finger strength by covering old plastic curlers and a board with opposing Velcro loop and hook material. The idea is for the player to pull the curlers off the board. Using both the narrow and wider curler sizes means different muscles will be strengthened.

Curler Poke

Here's another use for those old hair rollers. Hold one up and ask your worker to follow it with her eyes and poke a finger inside it when you say the word. This one is good for tracking skills and eye-hand coordination.

Beading

Threading beads is a great two-handed activity, and it can be done with a variety of materials. In the chapter on paper games, there was the beginner beading equipment of cut-up toilet paper rolls for beads and rope for string. The next level could be thread spools (painted?) and a shoestring. For the child who is ready for smaller beads, try buttons, short pieces of colored drinking straws, or macaroni.

Another beading material that's a big hit with children is Cheerios. They put Cheerios on a string and wear it around their necks, and then they have something to munch on the rest of the day!

Sewing

You can make your own beginner's sewing card with a sturdy piece of cardboard, a hole puncher, a good-sized blunt needle, and some yarn.

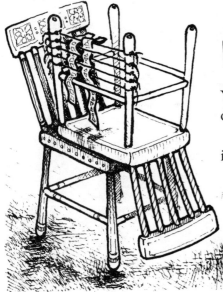

Weaving

You can make your own loom by turning a chair upside down and stringing yarn or fabric strips from leg to leg fairly tightly, firmly fastening each strand one to two inches apart. Then weave other fabric strips in and out of the warp.

Embroidery

You can make your own embroidery frame by cutting off the top half of a cottage cheese or other plastic container. Then take off the lid and cut a hole in the center,

leaving about a one-quarter-inch edge. Put some cheese-cloth or other loose-weave material on the container top and snap back on the lid. Voila!

Hardware Goodies

The hardware store is a wonderful place to shop for fine-motor toys. You'll find nuts that fit into bolts and hooks that snap onto rings and a lot of other things that go neatly together. They're great for getting small fingers working and young minds figuring.

Cheese Peels

A fine motor activity that is instantly rewarding. Use a potato peeler and a hunk of cheese and have your learner make himself some cheese peels.

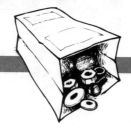

Fabric Dominoes

Make your own set of dominoes, or better yet, have your learner make the set, by pasting fabric pieces on cardboard rectangles. The game would be to match the material patterns together instead of the usual white dots.

Cork Drop

I've always hated to throw away wine bottle corks; they look so useful and feel good in the hand. Oatmeal boxes are another hard item for a pack rat type to get rid of. They are so colorful and so round.

So I combine them into a toddler toy, cutting a hole in the top of the oatmeal container and letting the child drop the corks inside. It's good for both fine-motor skills and eye-hand coordination, and if the child takes the top off and puts it back, she is also working on object permanence and motor planning! (See glossary for explanation of key terms.)

Glove Puppets

Cut the fingers off old gloves and have your player draw faces on them and put them on their fingers for puppet

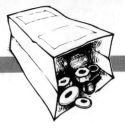

show time. Or they could draw the faces on cardboard ovals and glue the ovals to the fingers.

More advanced players can sew on fringe and ribbons to make hair and clothes.

Spool Puppets

Empty thread spools painted and glued together with added pipe cleaners for arms, yarn for hair and fabrics for clothes make funny people.

Paper Clip Challenge

To some fingers, fastening a paper clip to a piece of sturdy paper and taking it off again is a challenge. These kinds of activities are just right for increasing manipulating skills.

Poking Box

Isolating the index finger is a developmental stage of hand control that can be encouraged with a poking box. Take a thin box and make holes in the lid, a little larger than the size of the finger you are trying to entice. On the

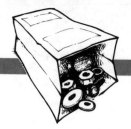

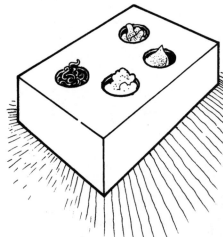

bottom of the box, glue things like cotton, peanut shells, sandpaper, and velvet scraps, in such a way that each poke of the finger brings a different sensation.

Hair rollers can be filled with material for finger poking, too.

Edible Modeling Dough

Dough is a wonderful medium for finger strengthening and increasing manipulating skills, but all too often it looks so good that children want to eat it. Rather than expend energy trying to prevent this, why not make up a playdough that's safe to eat. Here are some possibilities:

Peanut Butter Playdough
2 cups of peanut butter
2 cups of powdered milk
1 cup of honey
  or
Oatmeal Playdough
2 cups of oatmeal
1 cup of flour
1/2 cup of water
  or

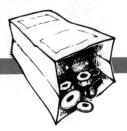

Homemade Playdough
$2\frac{1}{2}$ cups of flour
1 cup of salt
1 cup of water
1 tablespoon of oil

Or finally, use biscuit dough. Flatten out and have your child put his hand print on it; watch it baking in a toaster oven and then eat it up.

Edible Finger Paint

Finger painting can begin in the high chair or lap top wheelchair for the handicapped child who needs encouragement to use his arms. Use fingerpaint that is safe to eat, such as ketchup, mayonnaise, prepared mustard, thickened gravy, and so on.

If there is no danger that the child will eat the paint, here's a nonedible fingerpaint you can make yourself. Combine half a cup of starch and one quart of water. Add poster paint or food coloring or a natural coloring like beet juice or soy sauce.

If you like, have the child paint on a cookie sheet. It keeps the paint contained in one spot.

Try letting the child fingerpaint on a mirror. Then encourage her to swish the stuff around and find her face. I have also used plain corn-

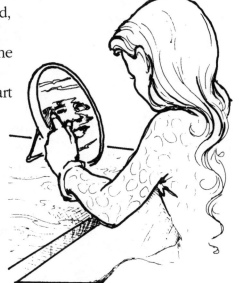

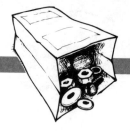

starch instead of fingerprint for this purpose and achieved the same effect with less mess.

Soda Pop Bat

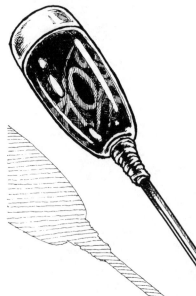

This is my all-time favorite bat. Take one of those half-gallon plastic soda containers and cut a dowel to fit inside the opening. Tape some duct tape around the dowel and bottle opening to keep it secure, and, voila, you have the niftiest bat or hockey stick or golf club!

Check out all the newspaper bat games (croquet, hockey, golf) listed in the newspaper chapter for game ideas.

Styrofoam Blocks

At last, a use for left-over styrofoam blocks, the kind used as packing material. If you have a child just learning how to hit a nail with a hammer, these blocks are great for holding the nails. They provide just the right amount of resistance to hold the nail upright but respond immediately to blows from the hammer. If you don't have a small-sized hammer, use a rock.

Try the same activity with screws and a screwdriver. Some physical and occupational therapists like to save those styrofoam peanuts used in packing and make

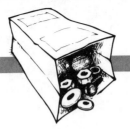

a bath out of them for children who need to increase their tactile awareness. I think it's a great idea, but I hate cleaning the peanuts up afterward. If this doesn't bother you, this is certainly one way to give those peanuts a useful second life. (It would be best, of course, if nobody ever manufactured them again: They're terrible for the environment. Shredded catalogs make terrific packing material, and catalogs are themselves difficult to get rid of, so two problems can be solved at once.)

Cutting Up

Give your child experience in cutting: Offer him a dull bread knife and food items like bananas, cooked potatoes, and hard-boiled eggs, or non-food items like play-dough or clay.

Cloth Toss

Pieces of material, especially if they are light, make great throwing games for the child. Have her throw one up and catch it, or throw it to another person or throw it so it falls on or covers a object.

Pieces of material can also be used for the beginning juggler, as they are slower to fall than balls and are

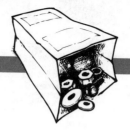

just right for children learning how to catch with one hand.

Painting

If you have chalk, a chalk board, a bucket, and a small paintbrush, try drawing a design on the chalkboard and asking your learner to paint it out with water. If you drew a person, for example, ask him to paint out the arms, then the legs, and so on. This activity exercises arm extension, spatial and body awareness, and eye-hand coordination, as well as being sloppy good fun!

Plastic Jug Toss

Cut the bottom off a plastic gallon milk container, leaving the handle intact. Put a ball of any kind inside the container and jerk the container up so that the ball flies out. Then try and catch the ball with the container.

This game can be played with two or more people in an unusual game of throw and catch.

Bleach Bottle Flip

Again, cut the bottom off of a bleach bottle or plastic gallon milk container, leaving the handle intact. Attach a soft ball, such as a large pom-pom made out of yarn, to a string, and attach that string to the handle. The player holds on to the handle, and by jerking it, gets the ball to go inside the container.

Sheet Target

Cut four or five holes of varying sizes in an old sheet. Hang the sheet from a clothesline or other support, and let your player use it for target practice.

It's fun to do this with two players, one to throw and one to catch. What makes the catching interesting is that the person waiting for the ball to come through the hole must be on alert. She never knows which hole, if any, the ball will come through, and must depend upon the rhythm of the throwing.

Sockballs are just right for this game.

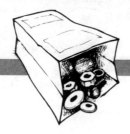

Thing Toss

You can help beginners gain experience catching by starting with things that are easy to grasp such as pillows, scarves, and rag dolls.

More experienced throwers can use these kinds of objects to practice catching with one hand. As they get better, throw two things, so that both of you are throwing and catching at the same time, or one person is catching one in each hand.

Squirt Gun Targets

Light a candle and have your player put it out with a squirt gun filled with water. A plastic bottle such as the kind shampoo or dishwashing soap comes in makes a great "gun." For safety's sake, of course, this activity requires adult supervision.

Have some extra candles ready if you want to play this game more than once. Wet candles are hard to relight!

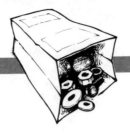

Balloon Darts

Pinning inflated balloons to a wall and having players throw darts at them is not new. It's a standard feature at any carnival.

What's different is having the players draw faces on the balloons with a felt-tip marker first. Besides encouraging more fine-motor activity, it can be psychologically healing. They can draw the faces of the people they would like to see busted!

Bird Cage Holder Targets

Once at a garage sale, I found a free-standing bird cage holder, the kind that has a metal circle on top with a hook. I can't tell you how many times I've used this contraption as a target to throw things through, or hung things on it for kids to aim at, or placed it at the far end of a balance beam with a bell dangling from the hook so that after a child crossed the balance beam, he could reach up and ring the bell, announcing his successful crossing to the world!

Throwing Games

Use a variety of throwing things for a child to toss in a sequence so that she can experience how different objects can feel to throw.

Possibilities include beanbags, sandbags, paper-stuffed nylons, tinfoil balls, newspaper balls, sock balls, masking tape balls, and balls made out of thousands of rubber bands.

Styrofoam Tray Hit

If you have two styrofoam trays, throw one up in the air and see how many times you can keep it aloft by hitting it with another tray. A girl named Annie came up with this one.

Styrofoam Hat Hit

Put a styrofoam tray on your head, tilt your head until the tray falls off, then bat it with another styrofoam tray. That's right, a kid came up with this one too. Thanks, Tyler!

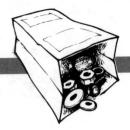

A Stone's Throw

If you ever happen to find yourself taking a child for a
walk over uneven terrain (great for balancing skills),
here's a game you can play when you sit down to rest.
It's an eye-hand exercise.

Gather some rocks into a pile or stack them in a
vertical line and then take turns trying to hit them from a
distance—depending on your child's level—with whatever
other rocks are handy. Any rocks that get hit become
property of the hitter. Continue the game until all rocks in
the pile have been distributed.

To make the game equal, the person with the
weaker or less accurate throw can sit nearer to the pile.
(Don't feel bad if that person is you.)

For fun, try seeing how many rocks can be hit
with eyes closed!

Different Kicks

Make a variety of balls to kick into an open box on the
floor. Point out that each requires a different level of force
to kick. Ball possibilities include: coffee cans, milk
cartons, paper bags with crumpled paper inside, sockballs, tinfoil balls, aluminum cans, and newspaper balls.

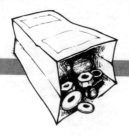

Balloon Kick

Tie a balloon to the leg of a table by a string. Let your player kick away: The balloon will never get out of reach.

Alternative Baseball

A fine game of solo baseball can be played using a tennis racket for a bat, a bean bag for a ball, and a figure eight layout for the field. The beanbag is easy to hit, and the figure eight run is a good spatial-awareness exercise.

Chair Fort

Put two chairs back to back and a few feet apart, and drape a sheet over them. Children love this little hidey-hole away from peering adult eyes, and since the space is small they get to be big.

Different Shoes

Collect a large variety of shoes for your player to walk across the floor in. Suggest different movements, like hopping, skipping, and jumping.

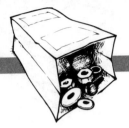

High heels, big boots, scuffs, shoe boxes, bags, coffee cans, and clogs all work well.

Wearing only one shoe increases balance sense as well as laterality, or "sidedness."

Palm Balance

In this game the player carries things on his outstretched palm from point A to point B while you encourage the techniques of good posture. Anything can be carried, from a peanut to a plastic cup of water.

Beginner's Balance

For children who are just learning how to stand on one foot, it sometimes helps to hold on to something such as the end of an unsharpened pencil while the adult holds the other end. I knew one child who gained such confidence in the pencil that just holding it alone helped.

Another idea is to let the beginner put the toe of the raised foot on the floor. If barefoot, the child can start with the ball of the nonsupporting foot on the floor and progress to the nail of the big toe.

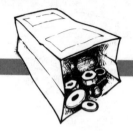

Balance Race

How fast can your child go when she's balancing something on her head. Try a variety of balancing objects: pillows, bean bags, oranges, and the old standby, books. Have a player try to beat her own time; or, if your working with a group, do relay games.

Pumpkin Walking

Needless to say, this is a seasonal game. Do you find that on Halloween there are always too many pumpkins and not enough things to do with them? A pumpkin of the right size for the feet you are working with makes a lovely balancing tool. Arrange the pumpkins in a line and have your player step carefully from one to the other.

Squash also works well for jumping over and around.

Pick-Ups

Place different objects on the floor and have the player stand with his feet a certain distance apart. The game is to see whether he can pick up all the objects on the floor without moving his feet.

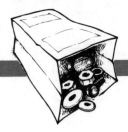

Change the distance between his feet to increase flexibility and balance skills.

MAKE YOUR OWN MUSICAL INSTRUMENTS

Making, then playing, your own instruments is a nice way to while away some time indoors. Here are some ideas for instruments and what to do with them.

Small Drums

Take both ends off an oatmeal or salt box and stretch a balloon across the top. Or stretch pieces of heavy rubber from an old inner tube over the open ends of an empty coffee can and lace or tie them tightly in place.

Tambourines

Fill one aluminum pie pan with metal bottle caps and put another pan on top. Punch holes around the edges and string the pans together.

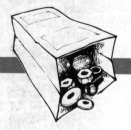

Or, sew Christmas bells to the edges of sturdy paper plates.

Wrist Bells

Bells are sewn to bands of wide elastic, and the bands made into bracelets.

Kazoo

Wrap wax-paper tightly around one end of a cardboard tube, fastening it on with a rubber band. Cut a quarter-inch hole near the wax-paper end of the tube, place the tube over your mouth, and sing away!

Shakers

Find two metal or plastic tops of the same size and fill one with beans, peas, corn, buttons, rice, or bells. Glue the second top to the first and then tape them securely together with duct or adhesive tape.

Xylophone

Use different lengths of discarded copper tubing or steel pipe of different thicknesses and lengths of wood. Lay them next to one another on top of a piece of foam, or hang each piece up like chimes by a strong fish line.

Or hang nails of assorted lengths and thicknesses from a board, using string.

Maracas

Put some pebbles in a juice can and close the opening securely.

Guitars

Make a hole in a box and wrap rubber bands around the box, positioning them over the hole.

Plunker

Tie a sturdy elastic taut between two nails on a board.

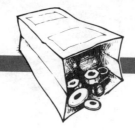

Games to Play with Homemade Instruments

1. Have children move to the sounds.

2. Have them move to the way the sound makes them feel.

3. Create a sequence for the player to imitate: Shake the tambourine twice, hit the drum, and stamp the feet.

4. Have child experiment with fast, slow, loud, and soft sounds on the same instrument.

5. Teach simple 2/3, 1/2, 3/4 beats.

GAMES TO ENHANCE GROUP PLAYING

Feather Blow

Get a group of children together in a tight circle, then toss a feather up above their heads and ask them to keep it aloft by blowing on it.

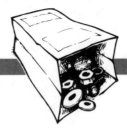

Mummy Sheet Wrap

Partners take turns wrapping each other up in a sheet, leaving the feet free for jumping around. Each wrapper is responsible for her mummy and takes it for a walk, trying to prevent any falling. This gives the wrapper some work on arm strength and gives the mummy some work on the leg strength. It's best to do this when there is a mat available, to protect children from the inevitable falls.

Caterpillar Walk

In this game, children get into a crawling position behind each other, holding on to each other's ankles; then you put a sheet over them so that only the first child can see. That child leads the rest of her "body" around the room and over or under a series of obstacles, such as mats and tables.

Variations:

- Make two caterpillars and have them race with each other

- Have a leader standing up directing traffic: "Head toward the back wall and then take a right turn at the basketball hoop."

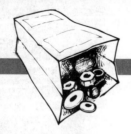

Serpent Crawl

This is like "Caterpillar Crawl," except that the children lie on their stomachs and squiggle to go forward.

Sheet and Ball Toss

In this game, children hold on to the edges of a sheet, and a beach ball or balloon is placed in the middle. By jerking the sheet cooperatively, the group tries to toss the ball in the air.

Once they have that technique down, divide them into two groups, each with its own sheet, and have them toss the ball back and forth to each other.

Ghosts

If you have enough sheets, one way to play Ghosts is to give one to each child and let them all wander around the room trying to find the others while making ghostly sounds. If the idea of children tripping and banging into each other doesn't appeal to you, you could have just one child be the ghost. The first person he touches becomes the next ghost.

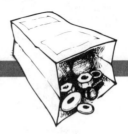

For adults, the idea of wondering around sightless may seem unappealing, but I found that the only "problem" about playing this game with kids is that there are always children who can't wait to be caught, and who make a point of getting in the ghost's path so that they can have a turn.

Kids in a Pocket

Another sheet game is to sew two sheets together on three sides, put a bunch of kids inside, open end up, and have the group try and get from point A to point B. Maybe you wouldn't enjoy it, but for many children this tumbling and squishing of bodies feels like a fun way to make connections with others.

Of course, there are some children who find this kind of closeness unappealing. Respect that difference and have that child or children stay outside the bag, perhaps directing it as to where it needs to go.

Big Beach Ball Games

If you happen to own one of those enormous, industrial-strength green balls, the kind physical and occupational therapists sometimes use, there are some great games you can play in a group.

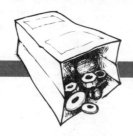

1. Hot Potato, Cold Potato, Bouncy Potato and Twirly Potato. Cold Potato means you gently throw the ball underhand to each other until a chosen leader calls out, "Hot Potato" at which point you begin to bat it at each other. "Bouncy" means you bounce it to another person; "Twirly" means you twirl it in a circle before you throw it. By the end, the players will have thought of any number of names and movements: squat potato, jump potato, kick potato. . .

2. Two people hold the green ball between their bodies; two other people go up to them and take it from them, using only their bodies.

3. Players stand in a line and pass the ball backward over their heads to the person behind and then return it between their legs.

4. Players lie on their bellies and roll the ball to each other using hands, heads, or elbows.

Musical Movements

If you have an assortment of musical instruments at your disposal, assign a movement to each sound. For example, ask the children to twirl when they hear the bell, jump when you shake the tambourine, hop when they hear the flute, and so on. Then play each instrument one at a time

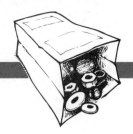

for random periods of time, so they really have to listen or watch to learn what you are going to do next. After a while, try playing two instruments at once so that children are hopping while twirling!

This game works well when you have children who are in wheelchairs, or for whom fast changes in movement may be too difficult. They can be the music makers, and you can be the director. Line up the music makers facing the dancers; you stand behind them and begin tapping them on the back when you want them to play. As long as you keep tapping, they should keep playing; when you stop, they should too.

Balloon Games

Although balloons don't recycle well, they are cheap and plentiful enough and wonderfully versatile. Consider these group games.

Important: Supervise all ballooning games carefully! The balloons can present a risk of suffocation. Children should never bite balloons or play with them anywhere near the mouth. Do not let very small children play with balloons.

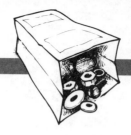

1. Have a group of players see how many times they can hit the balloon to keep it from touching the ground, trying to keep it up longer each time.

2. Vary the rules, so that sometimes players can hit the balloon only with one hand, or they have to alternate hands, or they can only use their heads or elbows or knees.

3. Have them try to keep the balloon in the air using water pistols.

4. Have them keep it up by blowing through straws or just blowing with their mouths.

5. Have them hit it with Ping-Pong paddles.

Balloon Train

In this game the group forms a train by holding a balloon between each person. How long can players chug along, staying together and not dropping any of the balloons?

Balloon Fanning Relay

You'll need two fans—the kind you wave—and two balloons. Divide the group into two equal teams and line the teams up single file. At the signal, the first people in line

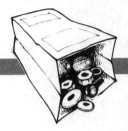

fan their balloon to a designated spot and then back to the starting line, where they hand their fans to the next in line until the last person in each line has had a turn.

Balloon Volley Ball

Set up a row of chairs to form a "net." Teams bat the balloon back and forth, and points are made if the other team lets the balloon touch the floor or hits it more than three times in a row.

Fireman Pass

An outdoor game that encourages cooperation and strength calls for children to line up and pass a bucket of water from hand to hand. Use this method to fill up a child-size pool, so that there is a logical reason for the game—not that children insist on logic. Or play this game:

Children pass the filled bucket down the row until it reaches the end person, who dumps it into a waiting empty bucket. Then she switches buckets, runs down with the filled bucket to the beginning of the row, and passes it down the row again for the last person to dump. This continues until there is hardly any water left. The idea is to see how many runs can be made before all the water gets sloshed out.

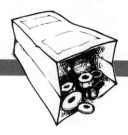

Two teams can compete, or one team can try for their personal best.

> *I think it's a good idea for children to know about this fireman's way of getting things done. I use it in my own home as a painless way of getting the firewood in the house.*

Clothes Relay

A fun relay race is to have a pile of costumes or oversized clothes at one end of the room. Beside the pile are two people who are the "dressers." The game starts with two children running from one end of the room to the other, where the dressers and clothes are. The dressers outfit their person, who then runs back to the starting line.

Variation: Have two separate but comparable piles, each with oversized pants, shirt, belt, coat, hat, and so on. The racer's job would then be to get completely "dressed" and "undressed" before racing back to the starting point.

The inclusion of dragging clothes and high heels adds the challenge of balancing while running.

Bubble Burst

Players stand around a bubble blower, who is perched on a chair blowing bubbles for the others to clap and burst.

CHAPTER THIRTEEN

Games for children in wheelchairs

Groups of children with differing abilities can all play these games sitting together. However, don't rule out using other games in this book just because they have not been specially designated for people in wheelchairs. If you want a mixed game with some children in wheelchairs and some not, you can include the kids in wheelchairs by giving them something to do within their abilities. Can they hold a hoop for others to run through? Can they point to the number that decides how many jumps are done, stop and start the race, or go through the obstacle course in their own style? With a little creativity and awareness, there is always a way for children to play together.

Sandbag Bozos

You know those inflatable figures that have sand on the bottom, so that every time you hit one, it bounces right back up? Toy stores usually carry them. They make wonderful equipment for increasing general strength and endurance. Bean bags or rolled-up socks can also be thrown at them, which helps develop arm strength. If you ask children to hit certain spots, such as Bozo's nose, then eye-hand coordination and focusing are also enhanced.

The toy can also be kicked to work on leg strength and range. Placed between two people or in the middle of a circle of people, it can be kicked back and forth or in different directions, making a social occasion out of the activity as well.

Hanging Balloon

Hang a balloon from the ceiling on a long piece of string. Have two players sit across from each other with the balloon between them and bat it back and forth. Here's another variation: Eileen, an occupational therapist, thought of making bats out of hangers and nylon hose for patients with more limited range. This game can also be played standing up to strengthen balancing skills.

Ball Toss #1

Tossing a ball around in a circle is not exactly a new idea.
Tossing two or three balls around at the same time, however, does add a new element: increasing attention span
and focusing. It's easy to "space out" when one lonely
ball is going around a large circle of people. If you do
use one ball, it's helpful to have the players call out the
name of the person to whom they are throwing the ball.
This increases awareness of others as well as memory.

Ball Toss #2

If you like the idea of tossing two or three balls around in
a circle, try making them differing weights, textures, and
sizes. For example, use a beach ball, a Nerf ball, and a
regular rubber ball. The differences increase awareness.

Cane Hits

Have one person hold a cane in a horizontal position.
Another person tosses her a beach ball or large Nerf
ball, and she hits it with the side of her cane. A third
person, perhaps someone who needs work on balancing
and flexibility, can stoop down and get the balls that
get away.

Long-Handled Sponge Soccer

In a stationary version of a soccer game, each player in the circle sports a long-handled sponge. A beach ball is rolled on the floor and hit from player to player, the idea being to see how many times it can be batted before it gets away. Or two goals, such as a cardboard boxes on their side, can be placed at two sides of the circle.

Bottle Cap Slide

Sitting around a smooth-topped table, players can flick bottle caps at a center target, or try to aim their sliding bottle caps so that they bang into each other.

Coins work well for this game, too.

Ring Toss #1

Ring toss games can be bought at a toy store, or you could make your own ring out of garden hose. (See chapter 4.) The game basically involves throwing a ring over a stick.

Because different children have different skill levels, what you need to do is to arrange either the posi-

tion of the stick or the position of the wheelchairs so that it's easier for the person with the lowest skill level and harder for the person with the highest. Nobody minds, I find, if things are arranged this way, and it reduces frustration and increases success.

To pick up those fallen rings, encourage the players to use reachers, long-handled tongs that increase a wheelchair-user's range. The practice they get using their reachers this way can then be applied to other areas of their lives.

Ring Toss #2

In this version of the game, the rings become targets. Lay out a series of the little circles on the floor and have the players toss small bean bags into them.

Socks and Buckets

Buckets and dishwashing tubs make easy targets for rolled-up socks or bean bags. Children can be sitting in a circle with the bucket in the middle, or in a line with the target moved to various places. The change in the target's position encourages the players to use their muscles in different ways.

Checkers and Basins

This is a step up from "Socks and Buckets," as it requires throwing a smaller object. Have players toss checkers into a dishwashing basin or bucket from varying distances away.

Target Shoot

Toy stores sell toy target guns that require loading suction cup darts or other "ammunition" into the gun (fine motor strength) and aiming at a target (eye-hand coordination).

Such guns usually come with a conventional target, which you can place on the wall, but I find that a hanging balloon makes a strongly visible target, and also makes a satisfyingly large movement when hit. Attach bells to the balloon for auditory rewards!

Can Bowling

Use aluminum cans. Set them up in a bowling pattern or stacked on top of each other and have the players knock them down with a ball.

Dancing

Dancing is a great balance activity, because stable partners can be chosen to pair up with the ones who have difficulty in balancing. The movements can be as simple as a two-step or as challenging as the jitterbug. I find that putting on the players' favorite music moves the spirit as well as the body!

Players in wheelchairs can hold hands with someone who is moving or be wheeled around in quick moves (upper torso balancing); he can also provide percussion sounds. A bag filled with checkers makes wonderful instant percussion.

Glossary

Listed below are the major motor skills that form the basis for good coordination, as well as a few related concepts that are important to understand. Included in most explanations are suggestions on how to tell when your child may need some help in one of the areas, and the type of activity that will help.

Balance is the basis of all movement. Balance is an internal awareness of one's center that enables a person to be quick and flexible in moving. As a therapist, I always check children's balance first to make sure that they have a good basis for building all other movements. If the balance is not developed, even walking can be tricky. Children with balance problems sometimes trip on nothing or fall out of chairs suddenly.

Balance games encourage postural awareness; these would be games like tiptoe walking, rocking, walking a balance beam, or walking with something balanced on the head.

Eye-foot coordination happens when the feet respond to information from the eyes.

You know how toddlers are when they first start walking. They concentrate so hard on keeping their balance and putting one foot in front of the other that they don't notice an obstacle at their feet. Down they go! A little later, they'll go around the obstacle, giving it a wider berth, perhaps, than is necessary. As their eye-foot skills progress, they will step over the object. Finally, they will learn to notice the obstacle well ahead of time, and casually step over it without even breaking the rhythm of their walk.

In other words, eye-foot coordination helps us to avoid tripping and stumbling over things in our path. Kicking games, leaping over hurdles, and stepping on stones encourage this ability.

Eye-hand coordination exercises encourage the hand to work with the eyes. Infants' hands flail around; when they hit or touch something, they look to see what they've touched. Because the hand leads the eye, that process is known as *hand-eye coordination.* As babies get more control over their movements, they decide what they want to touch and then their eyes "tell" their hands where to go. That's eye-hand coordination: the eyes lead the hands.

You can tell when a child is having difficulty with eye-hand coordination; they will tend not to watch what they are doing. For example, they might throw a ball to you but look elsewhere as they do so. As they engage in physical activities, they may seem distracted; that's because they haven't grasped the connection between looking at their hands and effectively performing a task with those hands. Verbal cues, given in a gentle tone, can be good reminders: "Remember to keep your eye on the ball." "Don't forget, you have to watch what your hands are doing."

Games such as throwing, catching, stringing beads, and bowling all help develop this sense.

Fine motor is a term that refers to the manipulation and strengthening of the small muscles of the hand and foot; at issue here is knowing how much muscle strength to use to accomplish different tasks. The child who always breaks a pencil point or tears through paper because he erases so hard may simply need some practice with fine motor games.

Fine motor skill development is the difference between someone who is "all thumbs" and someone who has "a way with her hands." Dexterity is more a matter of experience than an innate gift for a select few. Although it does seem that those who are born with long, slender fingers tend to have an easier time with small, sensitive movements, those of us born with short, stubby (let's call them "earthy") digits can perfect fine motor skills with practice.

Drawing, clay work, and shooting marbles are some activities that encourage fine motor control.

Flexibility is the ability to bend and twist one's body and to keep the joints limber. Children are born with good flexibility — but they can easily lose it if they spend all their time in activities that don't call for much physical stretching (like watching television).

The body is a very accommodating instrument. If you don't use a movement, you lose it. It is as if the body says, "Oh, you don't want to do that anymore? Fine, I'll cut off that ability; I won't waste energy on that movement." If you break your arm and have to wear a cast for a long stretch of time, you will find, when the cast is removed, that your arm has become stiff. You have to reacquaint it with its old motions. Similarly, people who have had a stroke and have to wear a sling, or who are afflicted with a disease that affects muscle tone (such as spastic cerebral palsy) must conscientiously stretch out their muscles — or contractures will form and calcify, and movement will be lost.

Flexibility keeps the body in a position to meet the various demands of daily life. Activities that involve stretching, fitting into enclosed spaces, or maneuvering through obstacles (by, for instance, taking a walk through the woods) all help increase flexibility.

Gross motor is a term that refers to the activities of the large body muscles. If our large muscles are well developed, they are good at pumping blood and fresh oxygen around — and they give us the strength to do the things we want to do!

Gross motor skills form a solid foundation for health and physical well being. Games that include jumping, running, hopping, and similar activities, whether for short periods or extended ones, help increase gross motor ability.

Group playing is the ability to interact socially on a nonverbal level. The idea is to have fun, learn about relating to others by playing with them, and, incidentally, develop motor and social skills.

Imagination may not be a motor skill, but I'm including it in this list because it keeps the mind in an open and flexible state.

Albert Einstein once remarked that imagination was more important than knowledge. He should know. Pretending, improvising, and acting all help keep the mind active, so that one sees the possibilities in life.

Motor control has to do with the ability to stop and start and turn quickly. Children who, when running, bang into a wall rather than stop before they get to it are probably having trouble with motor control. Kids who make a wider turn than necessary when taking a left or right turn may also need to work on this sense.

Games that encourage running and stopping quickly (such as freeze tag) help develop motor control. So do broad jumping games, because they give "feedback" as to how much energy is needed to move a certain distance.

Motor planning has to do with our ability to plan movements, even if we are only subconsciously aware of this planing. For example, a child who climbs a tree is displaying good motor planning skills. She must, after all, plan exactly how to get up the tree: "First, I am going to put my right foot on that first branch; then I am going to pull my body up by holding the branch above it." (Of course, she will also need good motor planning skills to get down!)

We all need motor planning skills in order to negotiate our way down a city sidewalk. We may not be consciously aware of it, but our mind, which has had a good deal of experience in dealing with journeys like this, is saying something like this to our body: "I am going to walk to that store, but first I need to go around that group of teenagers, step between the fire hydrant and the big potted tree, and then cross over that air vent." We have in our minds a plan, some strategy we carry out quite casually, without even any awareness that we had a plan.

Children who plow straight toward a goal — or right into people — without any apparent sense of the need to negotiate their movements probably need motor planning activities. Good games in this category are going through obstacle courses and climbing things.

Rhythm exercises encourage a sense of timing. Most people don't think of rhythm as a motor skill unless dancing or singing is involved, but it is our internal sense of rhythm that makes seemingly simple acts (like walking or running) look smooth. Speaking a language properly means mastering not only the words of that language, but also its unique rhythms. If we don't master those rhythms, our speech sounds strange to native speakers.

Even reading is affected by our sense of rhythm. Children who are just learning to read do so without a smooth rhythm; until they develop that rhythm they sound . . . like . . . this . . . whenever they . . . read.

Dancing, clapping, and jumping rope are activities that can help develop rhythm.

Sidedness (laterality) has to do with knowing internally that the body is made up of two independent halves. If you've ever seen someone who has had a stroke and been left with one side of the body paralyzed, you've seen vivid proof that we are made up of two sides that can each function independently.

Possessing laterality means being able to isolate the muscles on one side that helps us learn to hop; it means being able to integrate the two sides that help us learn to skip. It is this internal sense that some things are on our right side and some on our left that help us learn, for example, the difference between a "b" and a "d". Children who have difficulty with learning such differences may need to work on sidedness. Good sidedness games include hopping, kicking, and throwing activities.

Spatial sense has to do with knowing where one is in space and how physical objects relate to one another. This awareness helps keep most of us from getting lost all the time; because we know where we are in relation to everything else, we usually have a good idea of how to get where we're going to next.

Have you ever left a store with your child to head back to the parking lot, only to watch your child turn and walk in the wrong direction? Children with undeveloped spatial sense are the ones you don't trust to meet you somewhere in the mall or outdoors because you have a (justifiable!) fear that they will become helplessly lost. Games such as puzzles, mazes, map-making, and walking blindfolded help develop spatial sense.

Spatial awareness also means knowing how much space *you* take up. Remember, the amount of space a child occupies is constantly changing as the child grows, which means adjustments and readjustments are a fact of daily life. (Any woman who becomes pregnant must learn to relate anew to the predicament of ongoing changes in physical size.)

A child who flings her arms into someone else's face during play may not be being aggressive at all, but may simply be experiencing difficulty with spatial aware-ness. The child who never seems to bend down low enough to get under a gate or fencepost is probably deal-ing with the same problem. Games involving getting into small boxes, crawling through tunnels, and going through obstacle courses will usually help.

Developmental sequence of motor skills

Ages 1-2

Moves from sitting to standing
Creeps up stairs
Squats and returns to standing
Walks independently
Rolls ball in imitation
Pulls off socks and mittens
Climbs into adult chairs and sits
Uses rocking horse or rocking chair
Stops, starts, and changes direction while walking
Begins to creep backward down stairs
Builds tower of 3 blocks
Scribbles with crayon or pencil

Attempts to put shoes on
Unzips large zipper

Ages 2-3

Walks upstairs with little or no aid
Strings four large beads
Turns door knobs
Jumps from bottom stair, feet together
Walks backward and sideways
Walks on tiptoes
Puts on simple clothes with assistance
Throws ball five feet
Builds tower of 5-6 blocks
Turns pages one at a time
Kicks large stationary ball
Runs
Grasps pencil between index and middle fingers
     (rather than in fist)
Undoes large buttons and snaps
Unscrews jar lids

Ages 3-4

Copies a circle on a piece of paper
Cuts with scissors

Puts together 3-4 piece puzzle
Kicks large ball when rolled to him
Walks on tiptoe
Plays with other children
Runs 10 steps while swinging arms
Hops on one foot
Pedals tricycle 5 feet
Maintains momentum on swing
Climbs up and slides down 4-6 foot slide
Begins to somersault forward
Walks up stairs, alternating feet
Catches ball in both hands
Puts socks on
Unlaces shoes
Unbuttons clothing

Ages 4-5

Runs comb and brush through hair
Stands on one foot 5 seconds or longer
Runs, changing direction
Jumps over rope 2-3 inches off floor
Walks downstairs, alternating feet
Puts on own clothes when told
Opens up all fasteners on clothes
Walks balance beam
Pedals tricycle, turning corner

Cuts paper into pieces
Folds paper in half with edges meeting
Washes face
Recites own phone number
Jumps forward and backward
Bounces and catches large ball

Ages 5-6

Blows nose independently
Prints capital letters
Places key in lock and opens lock
Walks balance beam forward, backward, and
        sideways
Skips
Can copy small letters
Tells month and day of birth
Climbs steps of slide
Hits nail with hammer
Dribbles ball with direction
Cuts pictures and complex shapes from magazine
Catches scarf with one hand
Points to own right and left hand
Jumps rope independently
Rides bicycle
Hits ball with bat
Prints first name

Jumps and lands on balls of feet
Stands on one foot, eyes closed
Puts together complex puzzles

These are the basic skills; from this point on children begin to perfect these skills and become increasingly coordinated, depending on individual interest and experience. Remember that these are general guidelines. Children grow at their own pace and according to their own interests. Some children, for example, will be advanced in their finger skills, but slower in their large motor skills. Respect your child's current developmental stage; without pressuring, use the activities in this book to offer the opportunity to move on to the next one.

Index

If you have read the glossary and are interested in using games that develop specific motor skills, the following index will tell you which games develop those skills. For example, if you have a slew of cans and want to enhance your child's eye-hand coordination, just look up "Eye-hand Coordination" and see the games listed under "Cans."

Games to Enhance Imagination

Gross Motor Skills

String

Wood

About the author and illustrator

Barbara Sher, M.A., O.T.R., has been an occupational therapist for 25 years, specializing in pediatrics. She has written several books on children's activities, and has given workshops nationally and internationally. She has taught in integrated classrooms in Saipan, Micronesia; in 1992, she was awarded a fellowship from the World Rehabilitation Fund's International Exchange of Experts and Information. As part of this fellowship, she traveled to Hong Kong, New Zealand, Fiji, and Rarotonga, giving workshops to teachers, therapists, and parents. The Center for Intercultural Education of Georgetown University is currently sponsoring Ms. Sher in her work in Third World countries.

Janet Young has been a practicing artist for over 30 years. She has done graphic designs for album covers and a number of book illustration projects; she also does portraits and sculpts. Several pieces of her work are in international collections.